SONS OF THE PROPHET

SONS OF THE PROPHET

A PLAY

STEPHEN KARAM

NORTHWESTERN UNIVERSITY PRESS

EVANSTON, ILLINOIS

Northwestern University Press
www.nupress.northwestern.edu

Printed in the United States of America

10 9 8 7 6 5 4 3 2 1

LIBRARY OF CONGRESS
CATALOGING-IN-PUBLICATION DATA

Karam, Stephen.
  Sons of the Prophet : a play / Stephen Karam.
    p. cm.
  "Sons of the Prophet was produced by the Huntington Theatre Company (Peter DuBois, artistic director; Michael Maso, managing director) in Boston, Massachusetts, on April 13, 2011."
  ISBN 978-0-8101-2877-4 (pbk. : alk. paper)
  1. Lebanese Americans—Pennsylvania—Drama. 2. Families—Pennsylvania—Drama. I. Title.
  PS3611.A72S66 2012
  812.6—dc23

                                2012020225

Happiness does not await us all. One needn't be a prophet to say that there will be more grief and pain than serenity and money. That is why we must hang on to one another.

—Anton Chekhov, letter to K. S. Barantsevich, March 3, 1888

. . . it seems that in a little while we shall know why we are living, why we are suffering . . . If only we could know, if only we could know!

—Anton Chekhov, *Three Sisters*

I shouldn't be doing this, but I'm going to . . .

—Judge Gary F. McKinley, Kenton, Ohio, August 15, 2006

CONTENTS

ACKNOWLEDGMENTS

I wish to thank Anne Reilly, Peter DuBois, Robyn Goodman, Todd Haimes, Jill Rafson, Josh Fiedler, Chris Till, Ivana Eiger, Chris Carcione, Hilary Noxon, Betsy Selman, Carrie Gardner, Jessica Johnson, Dan McCabe, Jared McNeill, Charlotte Maier, Thomas Ryan, Nick Caccavo, Rachel Ayers, Julia Levy, Harold Wolpert, Michael Maso, Anna Kohansky, Bevin O'Gara, Jason Moore, Lisa Timmel, Charles Hagalund, Craig Lucas, Paula Vogel, Keith Bunin, Dan Sullivan, James Lapine, Robbie Baitz, NYS&F, Joanna Pfaelzer, Susan Blackwell, Gideon Glick, F. Murray Abraham, Marcia DeBonis, Saidah Arrika Ekulona, Dan Bittner, Carmen Herlihy, Jesse Austrian, Richard Poe, Audrie Neenan, Neal Bledsoe, Marceline Hugot, Lisa Kron, Michael Stahl-David, Brandon Dirden, and Sarah Coogan.

PRODUCTION HISTORY

Sons of the Prophet was produced by the Huntington Theatre Company (Peter DuBois, artistic director; Michael Maso, managing director) in Boston, Massachusetts, on April 13, 2011. The director was Peter DuBois; the set design was by Anna Louizos; the costume design was by Bobby Frederick Tilley II; the lighting design was by Japhy Weideman; sound design was by M. L. Dogg; original music was by Nico Muhly; the song "Come, Come, Ye Saints" was arranged /sung by Mark Abernathy; arm choreography was by Stephen Karam; the production stage manager was Leslie Sears. The cast was as follows:

Joseph	Kelsey Kurz
Gloria	Joanna Gleason
Charles	Dan McCabe
Bill	Yusef Bulos
Timothy	Charles Socarides
Vin	Jonathan Louis Dent
Doctor Manor /ensemble	Dee Nelson
Mrs. McAndrew /ensemble	Lizbeth MacKay

The play was commissioned and produced by the Roundabout Theatre Company (Todd Haimes, artistic director) in New York City on October 20, 2011. It was directed by Peter DuBois; the set design was by Anna Louizos; the costume design was by Bobby Frederick Tilley II; the lighting design was by Japhy Weideman; sound design was by M. L. Dogg; original music was by Nico Muhly; the song "Come, Come, Ye Saints" was arranged /sung by Mark Abernathy; arm choreography was by Stephen Karam; the production stage manager was Leslie Sears; the stage manager was Morgan R. Holbrook. The cast was as follows:

Joseph . . . . Santino Fontana
Gloria . . . . Joanna Gleason
Charles . . . . Chris Perfetti
Bill . . . . Yusef Bulos
Timothy . . . . Charles Socarides
Vin . . . . Jonathan Louis Dent
Doctor Manor /ensemble . . . . Dee Nelson
Mrs. McAndrew /ensemble . . . . Lizbeth MacKay

SONS OF THE PROPHET

Joseph, 29
Gloria, 59
Charles, 18
Bill, 74
Physician's Assistant, 40s or 50s, female
Timothy, 28
Ticket Agent, 60s, female
Vin, 18
Doctor Manor, 40s or 50s, female
Board Member #1, 40s or 50s, female
Board Member #2, 60s, female
Mrs. McAndrew, 60s

The roles of the Physician's Assistant, Doctor Manor, and Board Member #1 are to be played by the same actress. The roles of the Ticket Agent, Board Member #2, and Mrs. McAndrew are to be played by the same actress.

At the risk of stating the obvious, N.B.: all the characters are equally human. Eschew broad comedy. Gloria may say ridiculous things, but her mannerisms aren't ridiculous; Timothy has the occasional arrogant, off-putting comment, but he is still sincere in his beliefs, etc., etc. This also pertains to the actresses playing multiple roles—maintaining believability is more important than dynamic changes in voice or posture.

The set should be spare. The various locales should suggest human spaces, but not be burdened by realistic details. The play takes place in a pocket of Pennsylvania that's getting increasingly worn down; small towns whose identities were built around industries that are no longer operative. Cracked sidewalks, leaning porches, weathered siding. If the space allows, I say: let's see the back wall of the theater; expose the brick, electrical wires and sockets, etc.

A slash (/) indicates the point of overlap in dialogue. When it appears, the character with the next line begins his or her speech.

Words in brackets [ ] are expressed nonverbally.

Douaihy is pronounced: Doo - WHY - hee

TIME

July 2006–March 2007

PLACE

Eastern Pennsylvania

PROLOGUE

(Night.

A deer decoy sits atop the crest of a hilly road. It looks real.

Headlights appear in the distance, growing closer.

Closer.

Closer.

Closer.

Just before impact, the stage goes black with the sound of twisting, crunching metal.)

ON WORK

(JOSEPH *stands in a pool of light and performs a sim-*
ple arm stretch: an ulnar nerve glide. There's a kind of
grace to his movement; he has the body awareness of an
athlete.

Lights reveal his location: a modest office in Nazareth,
Pennsylvania. The room is expansive. It's also virtually
empty except for two desks. One desk is beautiful and
bare save for a copy of the New York Times. *The other*
desk is ordinary and crowded with office supplies.

GLORIA, *a well-dressed woman, enters with an Allentown*
newspaper. JOSEPH *stops his stretch, returns to the ordi-*
nary desk.)

GLORIA: Joe, have you seen these headlines? I'm beginning to think
Pennsylvania is the Alabama of the North.

JOSEPH: No, Gloria, did you get my e-mail? I need to leave early—

GLORIA: No, my Blackberry is busted, think you can fix?

(*She plops the Blackberry on his desk. The phone rings.*)

JOSEPH (*answering the phone*): Gloria Gurney's Book Packaging,
how may—no, wrong number . . . bye.

GLORIA (*engrossed in the newspaper*): With everything going on
in the Middle East can you believe the paper leads with a story

5

about high school football? A preseason look at who's the favorite to go to Hershey for the state playoffs . . .

JOSEPH: Yeah, well, football's big here.

GLORIA: I'm learning. I spent most of my life in Manhattan, so . . . I keep forgetting parts of Pennsylvania never made it above the Mason–Dixon line.

JOSEPH: I just need you to sign where I've flagged—

GLORIA: We're in Nazareth for the love of God, how can we be so detached from the Middle East when—drive ten minutes and you find yourself in Bethlehem, Jordan, Egypt, Lebanon, or any other town off I-78.

JOSEPH: Just need you to sign here . . . also, I need to leave early—

GLORIA: Oh of course, I thought you might need to, go, get out of here—

JOSEPH: Why would you think I might /need to—

GLORIA: Well because of . . . I heard about the bombing of the Lebanese airport, the civilian casualties—have you not seen the news?

JOSEPH: No, I mean, I've caught bits and pieces of it on TV, /but—

GLORIA: And that's exactly what Beirut's been reduced to again, isn't it—bits and pieces, God . . . so much suffering in that part of the world . . .

(*They both go about some business.* GLORIA *scans her copy of the* New York Times.)

I don't know how the Lebanese are able to endure so much pain, it never ends for them, does it? . . . and these images of Israeli tanks driving by Beirutis while—Beirutis sounds like a fruity candy, is that the right— /Beirutis?—

JOSEPH: Beirutis is the correct /term, I think.

6

GLORIA:—oh good, good, well . . . I'm sure your family agrees that Israel's, their desire to defeat Hamas is so /untenable—

JOSEPH: Hizbollah, I think you /mean—

GLORIA:—oh Hizbollah is, also, yes, as well.

(*Beat. They go about separate bits of business.*)

JOSEPH: Did someone tell you I'm Lebanese?

GLORIA: Well, you do share a last name with a young man who helped run the geography bee at Nazareth High this weekend . . .

JOSEPH: I see.

GLORIA: I joined the board of that foundation, I sponsored the whole event, so when I heard them announce "former champion Charles Douaihy"—Douaihy isn't a common /name—

JOSEPH: No, yeah, Charles is my brother—

GLORIA: Yes, well, I found that out after speaking to one of his teachers, so . . .

JOSEPH: I see.

GLORIA: . . . who also told me that your family was Lebanese, so . . .

JOSEPH: Yeah, we are.

GLORIA: No keeping secrets in Nazareth, that's all I'm saying.

JOSEPH: Right, but you realize I wasn't keeping a secret.

GLORIA: Right, but *you* realize I'm only bringing it up because . . . there were all these people at the event who were surprised I didn't know you had a brother, that's all I'm saying.

JOSEPH: What people were surprised?

GLORIA: Well, that's not the point of the matter, you're missing the point of the /matter—

JOSEPH: Oh sorry, wait—what is /the point of the—

GLORIA: The point of the matter is just that you shouldn't feel shy about discussing your family /in the office—

JOSEPH: No, I'm not shy, /I just—

GLORIA: No no no, I understand—

JOSEPH:—when I'm in the office I just don't like to discuss /my personal life.

GLORIA: Your brother's disability.

(*Beat.*)

GLORIA:	JOSEPH:
Oh I [thought you were going to say]— sorry, sorry . . .	No, I—I just don't like to discuss my *personal life* in the office—

GLORIA: I respect that, obviously.

(*They go about some business.*)

The, the only reason I even brought it up is that . . . and you may have already . . . picked up on the reason /why—

JOSEPH: Not really, what is the reason /why—

GLORIA: Well, Joe, here's the . . . even if no one's willing to discuss it, much of the publishing industry won't do business with me anymore.

JOSEPH: Who's not willing to discuss that?

GLORIA: I'm saying, Joe, you know where I'm coming from; you're a runner and—and with the knee problems you're having—we both know what it's like to be suddenly sidelined . . .

JOSEPH: I guess, yeah.

GLORIA: Yeah, yeah, we both know what it means to be on top, then . . . suddenly, fall from grace.

JOSEPH: I didn't fall from grace, I think I tore my meniscus.

GLORIA: I'm *saying* I was hurt you never told me—the teacher I spoke with, she mentioned your brother did a whole report about a *famous Lebanese relation* of yours, which is, Joe, that's all I've been trying to say.

JOSEPH (*genuinely unclear*): What have you been trying to say?

GLORIA: You are a blood relative of Kahlil Gibran!—the bestselling author of all time behind Shakespeare and Lao Tzu!

JOSEPH: No, no no—we're distantly related, as in our great-great grandfathers /were cousins—

GLORIA: I don't care if he's your grandfather's fifth cousin removed—Gibran's name sells books—why would you hide this from me?

JOSEPH: I wasn't hiding anything—Gloria, I am Lebanese. And my parents were born in Bsharri, but that's the extent of my Arabian heritage. Look at me, I'm white. We were born and raised in Pennsylvania. We're white.

GLORIA: Yes, but you're white in the same way a Jewish person is white, you see what I'm saying?

JOSEPH: What are you saying?

GLORIA: We'd pitch it as a family memoir: I'd hire the right ghost-writer, weave in Gibran quotes—

JOSEPH: There's no story, you'd have to make stuff up.

GLORIA: The best memoirs are fictional. We can work in your athletic ambitions—a former Steamtown Marathon champion—

JOSEPH: My training's on hold—

GLORIA: Then we'll work in the athletic comeback element—

JOSEPH: I might not recover—

GLORIA: If Lance Armstrong died of testicular cancer, would he have won the Tour de France?

JOSEPH (*"That makes no sense."*): No.

GLORIA: Precisely. The whole meaning of *The Prophet* according to Gibran is: "You are far, far greater than you know, and /All is well."

JOSEPH: All is well, I know. My father says that all the time.

(*Beat.* GLORIA *senses* JOSEPH *doesn't want to continue the dialogue, but can't help herself*—)

GLORIA: In Arabic, or does he speak /English—

JOSEPH: I need to get going, /I'm sorry—

GLORIA: Of course, no I'm sorry, look why don't you just ask your father if he'd be willing to—

JOSEPH: My father is in the hospital. He was in a car accident.

GLORIA: A car accident?

JOSEPH:	GLORIA:
Yes, I sent you an e-mail because I didn't want to discuss this in the office, so . . .	Oh my God . . . I'm sorry, you shouldn't even have come in—

JOSEPH: . . . he's stable—I was at the hospital all weekend, my uncle's with him now . . . /that's why I need to leave early, so . . .

GLORIA: Oh my God . . . of course, I'm so sorry /I didn't know . . .

JOSEPH: I'm fine, it's okay—

GLORIA: It's not okay . . . God, Joseph, what happened?

JOSEPH: He was doing maintenance work up at Penn State, and driving home he swerved to avoid—the police think it's some sort of deer decoy hunters use or—there's also a deer statue near Dunmore High School, they don't know—it was all smashed, so—

GLORIA: The Dunmore mascot?

JOSEPH: Well, /the police think . . .

GLORIA: That'd make sense, their mascot is—they're the Mighty Bucks, yes? . . .

JOSEPH: Yeah.

GLORIA: . . . though bucks have antlers, so if it was a deer decoy, a female deer, it wouldn't have antlers, I hope the police know that.

JOSEPH: I'm just glad . . . my dad could have died.

GLORIA: Do they know who did it?—

JOSEPH: Gloria, sorry, can you sign where I've flagged here?—this sets up the health insurance plan under the name of your business. And your Blackberry isn't broken, you just need to charge it.

GLORIA: Of course, I'll get that, here, go, get out of here . . . and give my best to your mother. How's she holding up?

JOSEPH: Oh, my mother is /dead—

GLORIA (*genuinely embarrassed*): Dead, oh God she's dead you've told me ten times, /I'm so sorry . . .

JOSEPH: It's fine, /don't worry about it . . .

GLORIA: No, I'm so sorry. She died of—it was cervical cancer, right?

JOSEPH: No, and /I—

GLORIA: Was it your aunt who had cervical—

JOSEPH: I don't know anyone who's had cervical cancer—

GLORIA: Someone had—was it your cousin who—

JOSEPH: My uncle had to go on oxygen a few weeks ago, I might have mentioned that.

GLORIA: That's what I'm thinking of, that's it.

(*Beat.*)

And how's your little brother holding up? God love him . . .

JOSEPH: He's fine.

GLORIA: The teacher I spoke with said he has a, uh . . . hearing problem, but maybe she meant . . . is it . . .

(GLORIA *picks up a paper on his desk.*)

. . . just noticed this handout on M.S., does he have—

JOSEPH: No that's just some scrap paper—can I please have that? Sorry . . .

(JOSEPH *puts the paper in the recycling bin.*)

Charles doesn't have—she probably told you he was born with one ear, it's not a big deal, he had one made out of his own cartilage when he was six, so you can't even tell.

GLORIA: One ear, what are the odds.

JOSEPH: It's not all that uncommon a defect.

GLORIA: Right, no, I'm just saying it's not as common as being born with two ears, is my only point.

(*Beat.*)

JOSEPH: What is your only point?

GLORIA (*answering her cell*): Hello?—one second, Joseph— yeah? . . . uh-huh . . .

JOSEPH: Your Blackberry has no power.

GLORIA: . . . great . . . okay, call me later, I'm talking with my assistant . . . bye.

(GLORIA *puts the phone down. Beat.* JOSEPH *picks up the phone, plugs it into the charger. They look around the room.*)

GLORIA:	JOSEPH:
You should know I'm clinically depressed.	I should go.

(*Beat.*)

GLORIA:	JOSEPH:
I'm on medication though.	Goodbye.

GLORIA: I'm sorry, normally I, I don't like to discuss personal matters in the office, I don't, it's just . . . ever since my husband's suicide, I've . . . did I tell you my husband /took his own—

JOSEPH: No, God . . .

GLORIA: . . . it's too painful for me to talk about, but . . .

JOSEPH: I'm sorry . . .

GLORIA: . . . he did, so . . . he grew up in this area, we built a home here, I thought moving back would . . . but for now his family wants to stay . . . estranged from me, so . . . I don't have very many /people to—

JOSEPH: That's fine.

GLORIA: Thanks, Joe.

(JOSEPH *is about to leave.*)

Oh, and can I . . . also . . . ask you . . . not to . . .

(GLORIA *gestures toward a bottle of pills, hidden on* JOSEPH's *desk.*)

. . . leave any kind of . . . medication lying around . . . I have a bit of a, I'm in recovery—

JOSEPH: Those are for my knee pain—did you take some of these!?—

GLORIA: I, I take others that counter the effect—

JOSEPH: That's not what I'm worried /about—

GLORIA (*starts to pick up some paperwork on* JOSEPH's *desk*): Is the knee pain why you've been doing all this /paperwork?—

JOSEPH: Just leave that—the business bureau's helping me and it'll be better for you tax-wise—

GLORIA: Why not let me pay you extra, you can buy private insurance—

JOSEPH: Because I have a preexisting condition that makes me ineligible to do that, okay? I *have* to get it through my employer so I'm, I'm happy to do the paperwork, *okay?*

GLORIA: Okay, I'm sorry. Go, get out of here.

(GLORIA, *a bit wounded, picks up the* New York Times *again, studies the images.*)

(*Half to herself*): So much suffering . . .

(JOSEPH *is at the door; he studies* GLORIA.)

JOSEPH: You'll be okay?

GLORIA (*nodding "yes"*): . . . and I'll wait to speak to your father about the book until he's—once he's recovered from the, uh . . . testicular can/cer—

JOSEPH: Car/acci—

GLORIA:—car accident, I know—God what did I say—

JOSEPH: Testicular /cancer—

GLORIA: Right, because, who do I know that had testicular—

JOSEPH: Lance Armstrong.

GLORIA: Right, that's it, that's it.

JOSEPH: My family is very protective of their history. They'd never agree to a book about their past. It's a bad idea.

GLORIA: Some people think it's a bad idea to offer full health coverage to a part-time employee.

(*Beat.*)

JOSEPH: That's irrelevant, Gloria, it was the major reason I accepted the position. You know that.

GLORIA: I also know . . . it's more than just knee pain you've got, right?

(GLORIA *takes the M.S. pamphlet out of the recycling bin, puts it on his desk.*)

You need health insurance. I need a book. You see what I'm saying?

JOSEPH: I have to go.

(JOSEPH *exits.*)

ON PAIN

(*A small doctor's office.* JOSEPH's *uncle,* BILL, *and brother,* CHARLES, *sit in the corner on two hard chairs.* JOSEPH *sits on an exam table. A* PHYSICIAN'S ASSISTANT *speaks to* JOSEPH *regarding his MRI films.*)

PHYSICIAN'S ASSISTANT: . . . the MRI reports show some clear deterioration in your knees, they're arthritic—

JOSEPH: Why is this happening?

PHYSICIAN'S ASSISTANT: You have hypoplastic trochleas—if you /look here—

JOSEPH: What does that mean?

BILL:	CHARLES:
Is this bad? What is that?	What's a hypoplastic trochlea?

JOSEPH: Guys, let me ask the questions, please. (*To the* PHYSICIAN'S ASSISTANT) Is this because of my running?

CHARLES: He won the Steamtown Marathon—

JOSEPH: Charles, /shuttup please—

BILL: Hey relax, /okay?

JOSEPH:	CHARLES:
Then tell him to wait outside.	I'm here to support you—

BILL: Calm down, we're fine. I'm sorry.

PHYSICIAN'S ASSISTANT: It's fine. You're the father?

BILL: The uncle.

CHARLES: Our father died—

JOSEPH: Charles—

CHARLES: It's not a *secret*, relax.

BILL:	PHYSICIAN'S ASSISTANT:
Okay, all right . . .	I'm sorry to hear that.

CHARLES: Thank you.

BILL: Hypo-what, doc? You were saying—

JOSEPH: Uncle Bill, can you let me do the talking, sorry—just . . . (*to the* PHYSICIAN'S ASSISTANT) . . . just talk to me, please . . .

CHARLES: I can't believe you say "doc" . . .

BILL: /Don't be wise.

JOSEPH (*to* CHARLES):	PHYSICIAN'S ASSISTANT:
Please wait out in the	I'm actually a physician's
waiting room—	assistant—

CHARLES:	BILL (*half in Levantine Arabic*):
I'm not waiting in the waiting	Hey, *habibi skot*—Charles, do
room—tell him to calm down.	you hear me? *Skot, ma tehko.*
	[Quiet, don't speak.]

(*The* PHYSICIAN'S ASSISTANT *isn't sure whether to address anything that's just been said.*)

PHYSICIAN'S ASSISTANT: The doctor'll show you the films, you'll be able to see the divots, the lines in the bones where the cartilage is being worn away—

(*During the previous line,* CHARLES *switches places with* JOSEPH *so that his good ear is closer to the* PHYSICIAN'S ASSISTANT.)

CHARLES: Can you say that again?

JOSEPH (*to* PHYSICIAN'S ASSISTANT): He can't hear out of his left—

(*to* CHARLES)

Stand still.

CHARLES: I am, Bossy.

PHYSICIAN'S ASSISTANT: I'm just giving you guys the rundown, the doctor will be in shortly—

JOSEPH: Could the inflammation be caused by something . . . else, some kind of . . . my arms have been feeling a little, I dunno . . . burning and . . . heavy? Kind of—I'll wait to ask the doctor.

PHYSICIAN'S ASSISTANT: Yeah, bring it up, and also—in your history you have your father checked as living, but he just said—

JOSEPH: Yeah, sorry, he died a few weeks ago.

PHYSICIAN'S ASSISTANT: I'm sorry. And the cause of death?—we need the history—

BILL:	JOSEPH:
He died because of some asshole kid—	Heart disease. Stop talking.

BILL:—some jerk thought it'd be funny to put a deer decoy in the middle of a dark road—

PHYSICIAN'S ASSISTANT: Oh God I read about this, /I'm so sorry . . .

JOSEPH: Yes but that's not—that's not how he died. A week after the accident he had a heart attack, the doctor thinks they're unrelated.

BILL: Of course it was related.

PHYSICIAN'S ASSISTANT: Does heart disease run in your family?

JOSEPH: Yeah, and my father's cholesterol was off the charts.

BILL: I don't like the way you say that, "his cholesterol was off the charts," like he committed a grave sin.

CHARLES: He doesn't mean it that way.

PHYSICIAN'S ASSISTANT: Did they find out who caused the accident?

BILL:	JOSEPH:
Oh, the police found the asshole . . .	No—please stop talking.

CHARLES: This is a sensitive subject—

BILL: The boy happens to be the star of Cedar Crest High School's football team. A team that's pretty competitive this year, so guess who's getting treated with kid gloves—

PHYSICIAN'S ASSISTANT: What do you mean?

BILL: Some former jock judge decides—right before he hands down the kid's sentence, the judge says, publicly and on record: "I know I shouldn't be doing this, but I'm going to."

PHYSICIAN'S ASSISTANT: Why would a judge preface his ruling /with—

BILL: Because he's postponing the kid's time in juvenile detention until after football season.

PHYSICIAN'S ASSISTANT: No . . .

BILL: Oh yeah, cited some bullshit logic about the "positive effects of participating in football"—

PHYSICIAN'S ASSISTANT: Unreal, and my nephew plays football for Berwick, so if anything I should be /siding with—

CHARLES: Please stop talking to him about this.

PHYSICIAN'S ASSISTANT:	BILL:
What's that, sweetie?	The school board has the power to stop the kid from playing. /You should write them a letter.

JOSEPH: Shouldn't we be seeing the doctor by now?

PHYSICIAN'S ASSISTANT: I'm sorry, he's very behind, was in surgery this morning—you guys can wait out in the lobby if you'd prefer?

BILL: No, no, we're fine. Thanks, Doc.

   (*She exits.*)

CHARLES: "Doc" . . .

BILL: Nice girl.

CHARLES: Yes, she's a nice forty-five-year-old girl.

   (*Beat.*)

BILL (*to* JOSEPH): Hey, what'd Gibran say? "The most massive characters are seared with scars." All is well, offer it up—

JOSEPH: I'm not offering my suffering up to the baby Jesus, Uncle Bill, I'm going to feel shitty about it for ten seconds /okay?

CHARLES: Hey, /cool it—

BILL: I'm saying be grateful—you have your health, you have us—

JOSEPH: *I don't have my health,* we're in a doctor's office because my knees are radiating hot pain all the time!

   (*Uncomfortable silence.*)

CHARLES: Can I have fifty dollars?

JOSEPH:	BILL:
No, no way.	What for?

CHARLES: A map of Indochina—

JOSEPH: BILL:
What do you need that for?   Indo-what?

CHARLES: To help the middle school kids prepare for the geography
bee, Angry.

(BILL *is laughing*.)

Don't laugh at me.

JOSEPH: It's too much money . . .

BILL: You laugh at me all the time!

JOSEPH: . . . use the games Dad came up with, those're free.

CHARLES: They're too childish—Somalia looks like the number
seven? /Afghanistan looks like a clenched fist?

JOSEPH: They work.

CHARLES: They work for five-year-olds . . . /Japan looks like a
snake . . .

BILL (*examining the paper*): Goddammit . . .

JOSEPH: What?

BILL: They still haven't published my letter to the editor . . .

JOSEPH: You mailed it yesterday.

CHARLES (*half to himself*): Russia looks like a headless dog . . .

BILL: . . . they *won't* publish a photo of that kid when he kills your
father 'cause he's underage, but they will print one of him when
it comes to profiling the top football players in the state? Give
me a break.

CHARLES: Slovenia looks like a chicken . . .

JOSEPH (*to* CHARLES): What's he look like? Did you see the photo—

BILL: He looks like a punk, shaved head, mulatto, wears a chain—

JOSEPH:	CHARLES:
That's kind of an outdated term . . .	Are you kidding me? Say half-black. Mulatto is offensive—

BILL: People call me things all the time, they always think I'm Italian or Jewish, I don't take *offense.*

JOSEPH: Calling someone Italian or Jewish isn't offensive!

BILL: Okay, he's half-black or do I have to say half-African-American, what makes you boys comfortable?

CHARLES:	JOSEPH:
Oh my God . . .	He's just some kid doing a prank—

CHARLES: And he's in foster care.

BILL: You're making excuses for him?—

CHARLES: If *we'd* been bouncing around foster homes our whole life, who knows /where we'd be.

JOSEPH: Plus, the stuff I did—when I put that gnome in front of Mr. Budash's driveway?

CHARLES: When did you do that? /Where did the gnome come from?

BILL: That was different . . .

JOSEPH: His yard. It wasn't different—

BILL: Budash deserved that—why would anyone want a plastic bearded man guarding their yard?

JOSEPH (*to* CHARLES): He could've been in a bad accident—

BILL: No one swerves to avoid a *plastic elf creature*, the black kid knew a deer decoy would make drivers—

JOSEPH: Stop calling him the black kid—

BILL: I'm sorry, the mulatto man knew—

JOSEPH: Stop it.

CHARLES: This whole thing has messed up *his* life too. He's really sorry.

JOSEPH: How would you know?

CHARLES: We chatted.

JOSEPH:	BILL:
What? When—	What does that mean, "you chatted"?

CHARLES: Online, he sent me a note saying he didn't expect us to forgive him, but . . . he's sorry and—

JOSEPH:	BILL:
I don't believe this—	I don't want you talking to him—

CHARLES: It's not your decision, I already did. He wants to meet us . . .

JOSEPH: We're not meeting this kid—no good can come of it . . . that kind of healing only happens in Lifetime movies.

CHARLES:	BILL:
I'll meet him alone then . . .	What's Lifetime movies?

JOSEPH: Television for women.

CHARLES: I don't need your permission to meet him—

JOSEPH:	BILL:
Of course you do—	Yes you do, you're not calling the shots. Just 'cause we never talked about it officially, doesn't mean that—Legally, I'm your guardian now, so . . . for both you boys.

(JOSEPH *and* CHARLES *stifle laughter.*)

What?

JOSEPH: Uncle Bill, you aren't my legal guardian.

BILL: Of course I am, who else—

JOSEPH: I'm twenty-nine.

BILL:	CHARLES (*laughing*):
Are you that old, my God . . .	Uncle Bill . . .

JOSEPH: How old are *you*?

BILL: Well I don't know what you think about, uh . . .

CHARLES (*smiling*): What, old man?

BILL: . . . what if I moved into the house for a bit? I'm thinking your dad would want that, just for a little while. Until this one's off to college—

JOSEPH: I've got things under control.

(*Beat.*)

How's your hip?—

BILL: It's fine.

JOSEPH: Yeah? And shouldn't you be wearing that little oxygen backpack thing?—

BILL: No, I just wear it at home, I don't like carting it—

JOSEPH: /But if—

BILL: Trust me, it's you boys I'm worried about, you with your hypo-whatevers . . .

CHARLES: We are turning into the disabled family.

BILL: Speak for yourself, I walk all over, you just gotta be careful now with all the colored kids /hanging out at the corners—

JOSEPH:	CHARLES:
Uncle Bill! It's ignorant to say something like that, it's embarrassing for *you*.	Oh my God . . . you can't ever use the word colored, are you kidding me?

BILL: I'm saying this to *you*—I worked at the plant for twenty-nine years—the moment Bethlehem Steel starts recruiting in Puerto Rico in the seventies, then the Dominicans came in . . . you think that corporation collapsed just 'cause of finances? The / plant could

JOSEPH: Yes, I do.

BILL: have lasted longer, your father shouldn't have had to switch jobs.

CHARLES: I'm *glad* he didn't have to work near a blast furnace his whole life, that's *progress*.

(*Beat.*)

BILL: You finish going through his stuff?

(JOSEPH *shakes his head "no."*)

JOSEPH: If I do too much at once it's [stressful and overwhelming] . . .

(*Beat.*)

BILL: How about the picture of St. Rafka, did you leave that up?

JOSEPH:	CHARLES:
Yeah. Charles . . .	No.

CHARLES:	BILL:
He'd find out when he comes over.	Why not? Put it back up—

JOSEPH: She's on her deathbed, Uncle Bill, she has no eyes in the photo—

BILL: Her suffering is what's beautiful /about it—

CHARLES: Right, no he's just saying an eyeless woman isn't fun to look at.

BILL: She was your father's favorite saint. He wouldn't want it in some drawer.

(*Beat.*)

CHARLES: I'll hang it up.

BILL: Rafka won't let you suffer alone, you hear me? Keep praying to her. All is well.

(*Beat.*)

CHARLES: We stopped going to church.

JOSEPH: Charles! /Are you kidding me?!

CHARLES:	BILL:
I don't want to lie to him—	Why would you do that?

CHARLES (*to* BILL):—it's a twenty-five-minute drive /and—

BILL: Oh well God forbid you have to spend twenty-five minutes in a car, Charles . . . *Mwarneh* [we are Maronite] . . . You want to know real suffering, take a look at your bloodline, the Maronites of the Diaspora gave their lives for your /faith—*Mwarneh*—

JOSEPH: We know . . . okay . . .

BILL (*shaking his head*): . . . a twenty-five-minute drive . . . Bobo and Momo would turn over in their graves.

CHARLES: You notice how our grandparents sound like clowns?

(JOSEPH *shoots him a look: "Leave it alone."* BILL *registers a cramp.*)

JOSEPH: You okay?

BILL: Yeah, just give me a lift, gonna use the restroom.

JOSEPH (*to* CHARLES): Go with him . . .

BILL: No, no, there we go, thanks.

(BILL *exits.* CHARLES *gestures for* JOSEPH *to shut the door.*)

CHARLES: Does Uncle Bill know . . . do you think Dad ever told him we're gay? I can't tell if he—

JOSEPH: No, he knows—

CHARLES:—he never talks about it—he still uses the word "faggy"—

JOSEPH: He's a devout Maronite, he handled it really well. (*Re:* CHARLES's *outfit*) Besides, did you even have to come out?

CHARLES (*re:* JOSEPH's *shirt*): I don't dress like a lumberjack if that's /what you mean—

JOSEPH: Please—

CHARLES:—that's why you don't date more, no one in town knows—

JOSEPH: People in town know I'm—

CHARLES: If people in Nazareth think you're gay, it's because they think you're a lesbian. You have to drop hints, /don't assume guys know—

JOSEPH: Charles, I know how to—

CHARLES:—no in this town you must drop hints; *you* get clued in by a guy's voice or shoes, /right?—

JOSEPH: Charles—you're worrying about the wrong things—you don't think . . . doesn't Uncle Bill seem less steady?

CHARLES: He's always used a cane.

JOSEPH: No, Dad, before the accident—he mentioned, he thought Uncle Bill'd be moving in with you soon.

CHARLES: Why?

JOSEPH: He caught him sleeping on his couch one weekend—it freaked him out.

CHARLES: Why would Uncle Bill sleep on his couch?

JOSEPH ("*duh*"): 'Cause he couldn't make it up the stairs.

CHARLES: Seriously?

JOSEPH: I dunno if I should say something to him, or . . . I dunno if I should wait or what.

(CHARLES *starts to cry.*)

Oh come on, Charles . . .

CHARLES: This is not good . . . this is not good—

JOSEPH: We're gonna be fine.

(*The* PHYSICIAN'S ASSISTANT *enters.*)

PHYSICIAN'S ASSISTANT: Guys, your uncle took a bad fall in the bathroom, can you come help?

(JOSEPH *and* CHARLES *run out of the room.*)

ON TALKING

(Bus station in Bethlehem, Pennsylvania. A few worn, plastic seats in the waiting area.

JOSEPH is in the middle of a stressful phone call, pacing. A prerecorded automated voice is at the end of the line—it is the ubiquitous female voice for most banks, doctor's offices, etc.

TIMOTHY—sharply dressed, handsome—talks to a ticket agent, having an equally rough time.)

TIMOTHY (*to the* TICKET AGENT): Is the storm really that bad? I don't want to wait if—

TICKET AGENT: All dem cars'r all panked up wit ice, youse gotta wait, even d'innerstate's panked wit snow.

(TIMOTHY *doesn't know what she said.*)

AUTOMATED VOICE (V.O.): Welcome to Dr. Manor's automated voice system. To continue, in English, please press "one."

(JOSEPH *sighs, he's been on the phone all day.* TIMOTHY *hands his map to the* TICKET AGENT.)

TIMOTHY: Can you outline on this map here . . . ?

AUTOMATED VOICE (V.O.): If you're calling from a pharmacy, say "pharmacy"; if you're a patient looking to schedule an appointment, say—

JOSEPH: Schedule an appointment.

AUTOMATED VOICE (V.O.): I think you said, "pharmacy," is that right?

JOSEPH: No, *schedule an appointment.*

AUTOMATED VOICE (V.O.): I think you said, "medical emergency," is that right?

JOSEPH: No—speak to a real person. Real person please . . .

AUTOMATED VOICE (V.O.): Sorry you are having trouble . . .

JOSEPH: I'm not having trouble—

AUTOMATED VOICE (V.O.): I think you said, "refill a prescription," is that right?

JOSEPH: Fuck you in your asshole.

AUTOMATED VOICE (V.O.): One moment, I'll transfer you.

(TIMOTHY *approaches* JOSEPH.)

TIMOTHY: Are you from around here? Could you show me—

JOSEPH: I'm on the phone, can you hang on a second—

TIMOTHY: Yes, sorry . . .

AUTOMATED VOICE (V.O.): Your call is important to us. Please leave a detailed message /and someone will return your call within twenty-four hours.

JOSEPH: Oh come on . . .

(*Sound of the "beep."*)

Hi, this is Joseph Douaihy, D-O-U-A-I-H-Y, I was supposed to get my test results three days ago . . . so . . . if you could just . . . 727-2538, thanks.

(JOSEPH *hangs up. He sees* TIMOTHY *with the map.*)

Hey, let me just do this now, let me see that map. (*Looking at the map*) Yeah, this is fine, what's outlined here, but the snow's gonna be panked down all along these roads—

TIMOTHY: Panked? What does that mean? Is that like . . . packed?

JOSEPH: Panked is . . . how you, I dunno, pank things down.

TIMOTHY (*smiling*): Like what do you pank down?

JOSEPH: Besides snow? Uh, you pank your hair down if it's sticking up.

(JOSEPH *starts to redial—then he notices* TIMOTHY *staring at him.*)

Can I help you with something?

TIMOTHY: No, sorry, I'm trying to think how to best say this so you aren't weirded out—I'm a reporter, I've been in town to capture some sound bites—I'm covering the board decision about whether to let that kid who set up the deer decoy /play football—

JOSEPH: Who told you I'd be here?—

TIMOTHY: No one, I just heard your name and wanted to, to say how sorry I am, so . . .

(*Beat.*)

I was told that your family isn't interested in doing interviews, is that right?

(JOSEPH *nods, not buying* TIMOTHY's *story.*)

I had to ask, sorry . . . good night, I'm just . . . waiting for the storm to die down.

(TIMOTHY *moves to a seat further away.* JOSEPH's *cell rings.*)

JOSEPH (*answering his cell phone*): What do you want?

(CHARLES *appears on the phone in his bedroom. A black-and-white picture of St. Rafka (in agony) hangs on his wall. There is Arabic writing at the bottom of the picture.*)

CHARLES: Is he there yet?

JOSEPH: No, the bus is delayed 'cause of the snow. You guys okay?

CHARLES: Uncle Bill's praying the rosary. Sorrowful mysteries. Kill me.

JOSEPH: Can you just say it with him? He'll be in a better mood.

CHARLES: I said I'd join him after "The Scourging at the Pillar."

JOSEPH: Good man, /I'll see you soon—

CHARLES: I've also been—can you talk for a sec?

JOSEPH: What?

CHARLES: So, okay, so Rafka is back on the wall . . .

CHARLES (*cont'd*):	JOSEPH:
. . . in my *bedroom,* Touchy . . .	I don't want her—

CHARLES: . . . and that Arabic writing at the bottom? Uncle Bill translated it for me—

JOSEPH: Okay . . .

CHARLES: "All is well." It means "All is well," so—I wanted to see what Gibran poem that's from so online, the first thing that came up is this hymn where—that's what's repeated in the chorus, "All is well, All is well," I put it on your iPod, it's in your bag just listen to it—

JOSEPH: No, not now are you /crazy?—

CHARLES: . . . no, no, Joseph, take ten seconds and *listen* to it, the song is—okay under the song, online, there was this scripture passage /that says—

JOSEPH: What scripture? Are you insane?!

CHARLES:—it matches Dad's birthday perfectly, 12:17—

JOSEPH: Charles, you can't keep /doing this—

CHARLES: "My son, peace be unto thy soul; thine adversity and thine afflictions shall be but a small moment." "My son, peace be unto thy soul; thine adversity and thine afflictions shall be but a small moment."

(*Beat.*)

Of *course* that could be *random*, but . . . finding it after . . . from the picture? . . . (*Pissed* JOSEPH *isn't jumping in*) . . . are you *there?*

JOSEPH: Yeah I'm in a bus station that smells like urine, I can't have an emotional moment with you now, /I'll be home soon, okay?

CHARLES: You're an asshole. Yeah, also I bought the Indochina map using your credit card, /sorry.

JOSEPH: You are such a shit, goodbye.

CHARLES: Bye you look like a lesbian *bye*.

(CHARLES *hangs up, disappears.* JOSEPH *notices* TIMOTHY *smiling.*)

JOSEPH: This better not end up on the nightly news.

TIMOTHY: No, and my broadcasts only reach the greater Harrisburg region, so . . . Some of the national networks are watching my reels, but . . .

(*Beat.*)

I really am sorry about your father. One of my closest friends, he lost his dad when he was ten, so . . . and like a year later his mom was in this bad motorcycle accident, which was . . . crazy . . .

(*A little awkward.* JOSEPH *stares at* TIMOTHY *a bit harder, making a connection—*)

JOSEPH: Did you run for Pocono Mountain?

TIMOTHY: Yeah—why did you—

JOSEPH: I ran cross-country for Nazareth High, you don't remember me?—

TIMOTHY: I don't think so . . .

JOSEPH: Really? I had good races against you guys. You were all terrible runners—

TIMOTHY: We were terrible runners. But our uniforms were excellent.

JOSEPH: You had excellent uniforms.

(*Beat.* JOSEPH *goes back to some business.* TIMOTHY *follows suit.* JOSEPH *thinks for a minute, recalls some of* CHARLES's *advice . . . stares at* TIMOTHY. *Who is handsome.* TIMOTHY *crosses his legs. He's wearing nice—possibly gay?—shoes . . . Beat.*)

JOSEPH (*cont'd*): You still live in the Poconos?

TIMOTHY: Oh, Harrisburg now, for work, but my dad owns Mount Airy Lodge, /so I'm back a lot.

JOSEPH: Get out. (*Lightly singing the jingle*) "Beautiful /Mount Airy Lodge."

TIMOTHY: "Mount Airy Lodge." Yeah, yes . . . I've heard that before.

JOSEPH: Fancy . . .

TIMOTHY: No, please, that's my dad's side of my family—my mom's side is blue collar all the way, my grandma still lives in this, this run-down house not too far from here, actually, so . . . I prefer to be with her for the holidays and stuff, feels more . . . real . . . than [the rich side of my family] . . .

(*A little awkward.*)

JOSEPH: TIMOTHY:
So do you—no, you go . . .   What kind of—oh sorry—

TIMOTHY (*cont'd*): No I was just gonna ask what kind of name is Douaihy?

JOSEPH: Off the record, /yes?

TIMOTHY: Of course off the record, yes . . .

JOSEPH: It's Lebanese. We're supposedly descended from, from French knights in Douai, France.

TIMOTHY: Chevaliers? *Je suis très impressionné.*

JOSEPH (*smiling*): What?

TIMOTHY: Oh [forget it, not important] . . . I, I've been to Lebanon.

JOSEPH: The one in Pennsylvania /or—

TIMOTHY: No, the real one . . .

JOSEPH: My dad was born there.

TIMOTHY: Really? *Btehke Arabé?* [Do you speak Arabic?]

(TIMOTHY's *Arabic makes* JOSEPH *smile involuntarily.*)

JOSEPH: Uh, *shway* [a little], /*shway* . . . .

TIMOTHY: Ah, *shway, shway*—hey don't laugh at my Arabic. How many times have you been?

JOSEPH: Oh, never.

TIMOTHY: What? Go, get on a plane, what's stopping you?

JOSEPH: Their airport just got blown up, /which'd make landing difficult—

TIMOTHY: Right now is not the time, but come on, you speak Levantine Arabic /and you've never—

JOSEPH: I just speak—I know phrases from my dad, and mostly—the Maronite services are in Aramaic mostly. My grandfather was fluent in Aramaic, Arabic, French . . .

TIMOTHY: Wow, what did he do for a living?

JOSEPH: Most of my family worked at Bethlehem Steel, /till it closed . . .

TIMOTHY: Oh, wow. And what do *you* do?

JOSEPH: Well I've been training for the Olympic trials /the past few years—

TIMOTHY: Wow . . .

JOSEPH:—unsuccessfully, /but,

TIMOTHY: . . . still . . .

JOSEPH: yeah, no it was a great experience, I came really close.

TIMOTHY: That's awesome. And now, do you still—?

JOSEPH: Now, I, uh, work for a wealthy deranged woman.

(TIMOTHY *smiles.*)

I have fourteen unread e-mails from her. (*Noticing a new one*) Oh, fifteen . . .

(*Beat. He puts his phone away.*)

JOSEPH: TIMOTHY:
I used to—   Is she—no, what?

JOSEPH (*a thought that amuses him*): No, I was [gonna say]—I used to have this image of my grandfather as this kinda woeful, uneducated guy—now I'm like: the skills he had—three languages, a practical trade, made extra money as a tailor—I went to college and the only marketable skill I have is stuff I knew before college, like word processing.

TIMOTHY: I'm sure he'd be proud to know you work for a wealthy deranged woman.

JOSEPH: True.

TIMOTHY: I'm sure he *hemmed the dress* of many a wealthy deranged woman in his day.

JOSEPH: Very true . . . man, I can't imagine what he'd make of . . . / nothing, no, nothing . . .

TIMOTHY: What? C'mon . . .

JOSEPH: . . . the man winds up with two gay grandsons, we're the end of the line—

TIMOTHY: Wait, *two* gay grandsons? What are the odds of that?—

(JOSEPH *sighs*.)

What?

JOSEPH: I get that all the time 'cause of that and now 'cause of my mom and dad, it's always the slowly shaking head in the grocery store . . . "God love 'em, what are the odds" . . .

TIMOTHY: Did your mom pass away /too?

JOSEPH: Yeah but /it's—

TIMOTHY: I'm sorry . . .

JOSEPH: No please, every family's got their stuff, right? The Douaihys have a habit of dying tragically. We're like the Kennedys without the sex appeal. I shouldn't joke about it.

TIMOTHY: No, but . . . (*gesturing to his head*) . . . you should probably . . . pank your hair down, it's all crazy back there.

(*Focus shifts to* BILL *on the couch, praying the rosary.* CHARLES *descends the stairs holding his own rosary. Dur-*

ing BILL's *prayer,* JOSEPH *attempts to place another call, then gives up.*)

CHARLES: Where we at old man?

BILL: Agony in the Garden. I waited for you.

(CHARLES *lies on the couch.*)

Is your good ear in the couch?

(CHARLES *sighs, sits up.*)

The First Sorrowful Mystery:

(*Reading from his prayer book.*)

"Jesus was distressed and anxious, and he said to his disciples, 'My soul is sorrowful till death; stay here and keep awake.' And going forward a little he fell upon the ground, and prayed that if it was possible the hour might pass away from him. Then he came to his disciples and found them sleeping. And he said to Peter, 'Could you not, then, watch one hour with me?'" . . .

(BILL *proceeds with the rosary,* CHARLES *lies down, facing away from* BILL, *almost in tears. Attention returns to* JOSEPH *and* TIMOTHY. TIMOTHY *notices a copy of* The Prophet *sticking out of* JOSEPH's *bag.*)

TIMOTHY: You're reading *The Prophet*?

JOSEPH: Rereading. My boss—(*checking his phone*)—seventeen— she thinks creating a product connected to Gibran'd be some kind of gold mine.

TIMOTHY: She's probably right in terms of sales, I mean with "The Prophet"—never before has bad writing been so richly rewarded. May I? (*Flipping through chapters*) Let's see here . . . "On Teaching" . . . "On Pain" . . . "On Death," here we go ". . . when the earth shall claim your limbs, then shall you truly dance." [I mean come on!] Did you highlight all the worst lines?

JOSEPH: It belonged to my father, kind /of a family tome, no, please—

TIMOTHY: Oh God, sorry, don't listen to me—

JOSEPH:—I'm just in search of /. . . [who the hell knows] . . .

TIMOTHY:—no, well he, Gibran comforts millions of people out there, so, I just resent he does it via . . . kinda . . . superlative youth-group-retreat-poetry? /I mean—

JOSEPH: Yeah, yeah—it's too easy, /right?—

TIMOTHY: Well the easy opposites are his genius—pain is joy . . . hard times are good times . . . agony is like a breakfast with angels, whatever—it's barely intelligible but exactly what a, a suffering world wants to hear.

JOSEPH: All is well.

TIMOTHY: Exactly . . . but man, as a reporter, the stuff I see on a daily basis . . . All is *not* well out there.

JOSEPH: You live in *Harrisburg* /—what's going down in Harrisburg?!

TIMOTHY: I'm saying, okay, okay, first of all I've traveled all over the world and secondly . . . I dunno, you cover enough stories . . . people's pain . . . it's their pain, whether you're in Somalia or the Poconos, it's . . . I dunno . . . whatever, this is a best seller, so— I'm probably just jealous. I'm working on a book of my own, a memoir about my travels, /actually . . .

JOSEPH: Wow.

TIMOTHY: Yeah, yeah, sort of a history through personal history approach.

JOSEPH: How old are you? And you're working on a memoir?

TIMOTHY: I'm twenty-eight, but I spent this last summer in Somalia —no one was giving me a chance to get out of local-beat stories, so I got on a plane with a fake press pass and a video camera—

JOSEPH: That's awesome, I want to start traveling /once I—

TIMOTHY: Do it, get out and see the world.

JOSEPH: I don't even have a passport, which /I know!—I know, I'm gonna—

TIMOTHY: Get one, you have to, until I went abroad and . . . camped out on a Somalian rooftop, you know . . . *walked* along Trajan's Wall—have you ever been to Moldova?

JOSEPH: No.

TIMOTHY: It's fucking amazing, it's this tiny country next /to—

JOSEPH:—it's in Eastern Europe, I know where it is. It's shaped like a foot.

TIMOTHY: It's . . . /I guess . . .

JOSEPH: Finances are a little tight now, so . . .

TIMOTHY: Oh, man I don't come from money—I stayed in hostels starting out—

JOSEPH: Your dad owns a casino resort!— /Liar! Liar . . .

TIMOTHY: I mean, I—okay, okay . . . I never *relied* on that, though— and I don't travel for *me* I—there are so many compelling stories out there that aren't being told and, and the fact people don't know about them, it . . . it compounds their suffering.

JOSEPH: Is that a line from your book?

TIMOTHY: You think I'd quote /my own—

JOSEPH: No, I'm just teasing—

TIMOTHY: It *is* a line from my book, I'm taking it out.

JOSEPH: No! /You don't have to—

TIMOTHY: I'm only writing it because—I do think bearing witness gives people's pain *life,* validity—

40

JOSEPH: Maybe it gives *you* validity—

TICKET AGENT (*over a raspy microphone*): Reminder to all a youse tuh keep cell phone usage to a minimum. Not everyone's interested in your personal business or world travels, et cetruh.

(TIMOTHY *and* JOSEPH *are a bit embarrassed.* JOSEPH *checks his cell phone again.*)

TIMOTHY: If you . . . go ahead if you need to get back to—

JOSEPH: Yeah, no sorry I'm just—expecting a call . . .

(*He puts his phone away.*)

I didn't realize the whole doctor system, the way you have to advocate for yourself—I'm young, I can do it, but my uncle—the production it took to get Medicare to cover his wheelchair—it was like a full-time job for three people.

TIMOTHY: Yikes. This buddy I went to school with in New Haven was in a wheelchair for a whole semester, he got Crohn's disease, needed to have his whole intestine removed.

JOSEPH: Oh /man.

TIMOTHY: Yeah, yeah, and he was probably the guy I was closest to my freshman year. Yale had an amazing disability office, though, really /supportive.

JOSEPH: Good, good . . .

TIMOTHY: And you—you got the wheelchair in the end? For your— /uncle?

JOSEPH: Yeah. The real fun was—we had to convert our downstairs closet into like a half-bathroom, but—you can't shut the door, the toilet takes up too much space, so my uncle now shouts to warn us any time he's on the can, which is as glorious as it sounds.

TIMOTHY: And what's going on with *you*?

JOSEPH: Nothing hopefully, I got this one test result that was a little off so now I'm waiting on other results that'll rule out—they keep saying "something more global," rule out something *global*.

TIMOTHY: Do they know you don't even have a passport?

(JOSEPH *smiles.*)

Well, I hope you can just chill out until you get the results, let your family take care of you.

JOSEPH: My family's—even my father, the best guy, right?—but if I was diagnosed with something like M.S., he'd comfort me by saying: "Joseph, you should be grateful you *have* a central nervous system for your body to attack . . . do you know how many people have bodies that aren't *healthy* enough to attack their own central nervous system?"

(TIMOTHY *smiles.*)

Even—the only TV show we watched together growing up? "Little House on the Prairie," where God-fearing people /suffer with a smile—

TIMOTHY: I loved that show . . .

JOSEPH: Sure, but—was there anything the Ingalls didn't have to go through? Especially Mary Ingalls, I mean—

TIMOTHY: Mary definitely got the short end of the stick. I hated when she went blind—

JOSEPH: She goes blind, which is bad enough when you're living in the eighteen-somethings and you're dirt poor, right? But then—

TIMOTHY: Her baby dies!

JOSEPH: Her baby *burns alive in a fire!*—

TIMOTHY: Didn't she also get kicked by a skittish horse?

JOSEPH: Yes! Mary needed surgery after that she had internal bleeding—and of course her father, he can't afford the operation—

TIMOTHY: He's a mill-worker-farm guy, he can't afford that . . .

JOSEPH: So he goes to work on the railroad to fund the surgery and he gets *blasted* by /dynamite!

TIMOTHY: Dynamite! Oh my God . . . oh man . . .

(*They recover.* JOSEPH's *cell rings.*)

Doctor?

JOSEPH: No. Boss.

(JOSEPH *screens the call.*)

I think Almonzo was my first crush, remember Almonzo?

TIMOTHY: Yeah. I had an Almonzo phase.

(*Beat.*)

Was coming out in your family . . . I mean, Maronites . . .

JOSEPH: I wasn't dreaming of a Phalangist wedding or anything, so no big story to tell there. You? Or should I just read about it in your memoir?

TIMOTHY: Ha, no—it's not a secret, but with my profession and everything, I just don't discuss it.

JOSEPH: Not even a mention?

TIMOTHY: In life, yes, but in my book? No. That part of me is private.

JOSEPH: Then why are you writing a *memoir*?

TIMOTHY: If I need the trust of people in third world countries I can't comment on—

JOSEPH: But you *will* comment on your grandmother's . . . poverty /or whatever?

TIMOTHY: She's blue collar and

TIMOTHY:	JOSEPH:
that's different, that's— honestly, your points are— they're not fair.	I'm sorry, I'm playing devil's advocate because—

JOSEPH: I think they're fair points to *consider*—

TIMOTHY: Oh, okay, sure.

JOSEPH: Yes, correct.

TIMOTHY: Exactly, then. Sure.

JOSEPH: Are you *fake*-agreeing with me?

TICKET AGENT (*over a raspy microphone*): Hey ladies, dinnerstates clear, the plows got through.

(TIMOTHY *gets up to leave.*)

JOSEPH: You off?

TIMOTHY: Yeah, the station's putting me up in some shitty Hampton Inn for the night. Yay.

JOSEPH: The one in Easton? Please, it has a hot tub and free continental breakfast, it's completely classy.

(TIMOTHY *smiles.*)

Hey . . . [level with me] . . . how did you know I'd be here? Did someone tell you *who* I'm waiting for—

TIMOTHY: Wow, you're paranoid. No one, okay? Okay?

(JOSEPH *sighs, relieved.*)

JOSEPH: Okay.

(TIMOTHY *goes to leave. Stops, sighs.*)

TIMOTHY (*a confession*): Your brother updated his status online, said you were at the bus station waiting to /pick up—

JOSEPH: You're monitoring /my family's online activity?!—oh my God . . . fuck you, dude . . . I'm gonna kill Charles . . .

TIMOTHY: I'm sorry, I got caught in my own lies—I liked you so—

JOSEPH: Why didn't you just /tell me?—

TIMOTHY: Because—I'm telling you *now*—

JOSEPH: Yeah, well good night. /Goodbye—

TIMOTHY: Joseph—

TICKET AGENT: Reminder that loud cell phone conversation is strictly prohibited, thanks.

(JOSEPH *sits, upset.* TIMOTHY *goes to leave, but stops. Returns. Hands* JOSEPH *a business card.*)

TIMOTHY: Look, just . . . please take this in case you ever, uh . . . if you ever wanna talk or if . . . if your family ever decides to talk to the press—

JOSEPH: Wow, okay, goodbye.

TIMOTHY: I didn't /mean—

JOSEPH: Good night.

(TIMOTHY *exits.* JOSEPH *stares at* TIMOTHY'*s business card. He tosses it on the floor.* JOSEPH *thinks, gets headphones /iPod out of his bag.*

An acoustic rock guitar version of the hymn "Come, Come, Ye Saints" sounds.

"Come, Come, Ye Saints" comes to the forefront as a young man enters the bus station. This is VIN. JOSEPH *doesn't notice him.* VIN *tentatively approaches him as the stage transforms into . . .*)

ON HOME

(*. . . the Douaihy home.* CHARLES, VIN, *and* JOSEPH *sit on the couch in the Douaihy living room. They look away from a makeshift bathroom, toward a small Christmas tree that should have a few more ornaments and lights on it.*

The bathroom is a converted closet, so there isn't room for a person to sit on the toilet and shut the door. We see BILL's *feet sticking out of the doorway. Sounds of urinating.*

There is a walker with a built-in seat near the bathroom door. A hospital bed sits awkwardly in the room (metal rails on each side). The sound of a toilet flush. VIN *is uncomfortable.* BILL *emerges from the makeshift bathroom, signals to* JOSEPH *he doesn't need his help. Using the walker,* BILL *makes his way back to the couch area. Everyone can now face a more comfortable direction.*)

VIN: I like the tree.

CHARLES:
Thanks.

BILL:
It's the worst Christmas tree I've ever had. But that's because I had to do everything myself . . .

JOSEPH: /I bought the tree, dragged it home and set it up how is that—

BILL: . . . none of these guys wanted to help this year, what are you gonna do? My brother always had the tree up right after Thanksgiving. Your family have a tree? Or do you not celebrate—

(CHARLES *sighs audibly.*)

—what are you sighing about—I don't know if he's Christian or what, I'm just asking.

VIN: The foster people I'm with aren't religious but they have a tree.

JOSEPH:	BILL:
Do you—	One of my buddies at the American Legion knows them, I did some asking around—

JOSEPH: He wasn't snooping, just curious—

BILL: He knows. It was nice to hear, a white couple taking in a black kid, /that's encouraging—

JOSEPH:	CHARLES (*to* VIN):
Uncle Bill, we agreed we were gonna let Vin talk to *us* first—	He's from a generation where—

BILL: I am saying I think it's a good thing, it's *encouraging* to know . . .

VIN (*to* JOSEPH): It's cool.

BILL (*to* VIN): Just because I'm not PC doesn't mean—my father moved us here penniless, Vin, I know what it's like to be a fish out of water. We were in the northeast, West Scranton, this is before your dad moved you to Moscow . . .

VIN: Where's Moscow?

CHARLES:	BILL:
Northeast PA.	. . . and we grew up sleeping on mattresses . . .

JOSEPH: Okay, /Uncle Bill.

BILL: . . . we didn't wait for handouts when we arrived here, /but today there's pockets of immigrants . . .

CHARLES: Oh my God . . .

BILL: I'm not saying hard work isn't in their blood, but now they expect a free ride—ESL programs, Mexican parade—

JOSEPH:	BILL:
Uncle Bill, let Vin—	—all our tax dollars—I'm just saying that keeps happening, what's the identity of America going to be?

CHARLES: That *is* the identity of America, you're making no sense.

JOSEPH: What happened to the pride you said Bobo felt to live in a country so American it has Lebanon as its center?

VIN: Center of what?

CHARLES: Lebanon, Kansas, is the geodetic center of the U.S. /it's the . . .

JOSEPH (*to* CHARLES): He won't know what "geodetic" means—(*to* VIN)—he's a geography /buff . . .

CHARLES: I'll explain it to him, Anxious, if you stop interrupting me—

BILL: Right in the heart of this country, in Kansas, is a town called Lebanon, in the exact center, what are the odds of that? Bobo saw that on a map, knew it was a sign . . .

CHARLES (*to* VIN): Obviously the center of a country is—it's an emotional realm, mathematically there is no [such thing]—

VIN: Wait—who's Bobo?

JOSEPH: CHARLES:
Our grandfather. (*To* CHARLES)   A circus clown.
Don't do that.

BILL: Every week now, Vin—(*to* JOSEPH, *who has put his hand on* BILL's *arm to quiet him*)—let me tell him this, 'cause of this war, there's thousands of Maronites coming over; no money, starting from scratch—it's like when I was a boy, none of us spoke English and my brother—

CHARLES: We know—

BILL: I'm telling Vin, he should know something about the man he killed.

(*Small beat*—)

CHARLES: JOSEPH:
We don't /think—   That's, that's not how we
                                    see it . . . (*upset, to* BILL,
                                    "Why are you doing this?")
                                    Uncle Bill.

VIN: No, let him—you can say whatever.

(JOSEPH *adjusts* BILL's *oxygen backpack, puts the tubes in his nose.*)

BILL: JOSEPH:
Their father, he was the   Don't get worked up, let's
smartest kid in his class,   just . . . put this back on
he was teaching *us*   while we're talking, here . . .
English. (*To* VIN) And I'm
not prejudiced, these guys
know, they're minorities. I even
joined that human equality
nonsense for these two.

VIN: Wait, is one of you gay?

| JOSEPH: | CHARLES: |
| Both of us. | We both are. |

VIN: Seriously?—

JOSEPH: Look, Vin, do you /wanna—

VIN: I brought the—I brought the essay the judge asked me to write. (*Taking out the essay, to* JOSEPH) /Is it all right if . . . ?

JOSEPH: You're gonna—oh of course.

VIN (*nervous, reading*): "I'm very sorry. I know what I did was wrong. I think every day that I hurt someone and will always remember the negative effect my actions had on others. Insulting the Dunmore mascot was something I was dared to do by my team but was ultimately my decision to do it and so I'm deeply sorry and will think about my actions for a long time to come and won't repeat them. Letting people—I hope that by saying this and letting people know it was wrong, my actions will be seen as not intentional to hurt someone, but ignorant and never intended to hurt anyone. Hurting someone though is what I did and so I will feel that inside every day when I wake and have to live with that." That's obviously, like, 200 words, I need to have 500. Can't believe how nervous I am.

BILL: This shouldn't be easy for you.

VIN: Sorry, I'm—I dunno if you know that if—even if the school board decides to stop me from playing next week, there's only gonna be one playoff game left—three if we keep winning, so . . . my coach thought, you know . . .

BILL: If you're here to say you're gonna withdraw from the team, you'd be a big man.

(*Uncomfortable beat.*)

VIN:	JOSEPH:
I think—	We don't—[no, go ahead, finish . . .]

VIN: I think what the judge was thinking is . . . [Look,] my grades are decent. But football's the way I'm going somewhere on *scholar-ship* and somewhere *good*, so . . . that's what the judge was thinking about, I think, with his decision?

(*Uncomfortable beat.*)

/So my—

JOSEPH: Are you—no, go on . . .

VIN: So I dunno if . . . you guys . . . put in a good word for me . . . obviously then . . . you know . . .

(*Beat.* CHARLES *checks in with* JOSEPH *about this.*)

I'm really sorry, seriously. I don't sleep most nights, I literally have bad dreams.

BILL: You literally have bad dreams? Seriously? /Do you know what you've *literally* taken from this family? . . . that son-of-a-bitch is gonna stop my heart . . .

JOSEPH: Breathe through your nose—calm down, calm down . . . (*to* CHARLES)—take Vin upstairs for a few minutes, Charles—*do it,* /okay?

CHARLES:	BILL:
Don't tell me what to do. (*To* BILL) Uncle Bill, chill out.	What did you think would happen when you put that thing in the middle of the road?!

JOSEPH:	VIN (*to* BILL):
Just go upstairs guys—	I'm sorry.

BILL: How about an essay /called "Why I am dumb jock and I'll never have to think about the repercussions of my actions"— (*registering a cramp*)—dammit . . .

CHARLES:	JOSEPH:
Don't listen to him . . . this is so embarrassing . . . (*To* BILL) Please chill out.	Let's go in the kitchen . . . all right, calm down . . . *go upstairs*—

(CHARLES *sighs, heads for the stairs.* VIN *follows.*)

CHARLES: C'mon . . .

VIN:	BILL:
Should I bring my bag?	Dammit, I have to use the bathroom . . .

CHARLES: Yeah.

(VIN *picks up his bag.*)

Your arms are huge . . .

JOSEPH: Breathe through your nose . . . /breathe through your nose . . .

VIN: I lift three times a week.

(*Doorbell rings.*)

JOSEPH:	CHARLES:
Who the hell is that?	Say it again? This ear is no good.

BILL:	VIN:
Don't push me.	What's wrong with your ear?

CHARLES: It's fake—they made it outta a piece of my rib, /you can still see the scar . . .

(*The doorbell rings.*)

JOSEPH: Charles—Charles! Did you invite someone over?

CHARLES: No, Snapper . . .

BILL: Can you /get the door?

VIN: Is it like /plastic or what is it?

CHARLES (*to* VIN, *starting up the stairs*): Just touch it, feel it it's skin . . .

> (*The doorbell rings.* CHARLES *takes* VIN's *hand, puts it in his ear.*)

VIN:	JOSEPH (*calling to the door*):
That is so weird. Where'd the skin come from?	One minute! (*Walking* BILL *to the open bathroom*) Breathe through your nose . . .
CHARLES:	JOSEPH:
From my chest, here . . . [I'll show you] . . .	Breathe through your /nose—

BILL: *You* breathe through your nose, I'm fine.

> (*The doorbell rings.*)

JOSEPH:	BILL:
I'm coming!	Don't open the door until I'm finished going.

CHARLES (*stopping midstairs*): You can feel the scar if you want—

> (CHARLES *puts* VIN's *hand on his scar.* JOSEPH *catches a glimpse of this on his way to answer the door.*)

JOSEPH: What the hell are you doing?! Go upstairs!

CHARLES: We're *fine.*

> (JOSEPH *waits until* VIN *and* CHARLES *are out of view, then opens the door.* GLORIA *stands outside.*)

GLORIA: Don't be upset, Joe, I was alone and I—

JOSEPH: Gloria, /what are you doing here?—

GLORIA: I'm sorry, I know I'm surprising you, is this a bad time? /
Can I just—

JOSEPH: It is, I'm sorry, are you okay? /What's wrong?—

GLORIA: Can I just stay five minutes, I had a bit of a . . . you weren't
answering your phone and I . . .

JOSEPH: How about I call you—Gloria can you please . . . [not walk into my house] . . . Gloria, how about I call you in an hour, okay?	GLORIA (*sees the living room*): I uh . . . sorry, I'm just, wow, noticing . . . all of the . . .

GLORIA: . . . look at how beautiful your home is . . . and look at all
these . . . afghans and . . . throws on all the furniture . . . wow . . .

(*Noises of urinating from the bathroom.* JOSEPH *moves*
GLORIA *further into the living room.*)

JOSEPH: Can you just come over here for a sec . . . my uncle, we had
to build him a temporary bathroom in our closet, he can't go up
steps, so—

GLORIA: Oh, God love him . . .

(*Toilet flushes.*)

JOSEPH: I'm sorry to be so blunt, but you can't stay—

GLORIA: I have good news about our project, there was a sign in
today's paper . . .

JOSEPH: Can this wait until /tomorrow? Now is—

BILL: Joseph . . . ?

(JOSEPH *guides him to his walker.*)

JOSEPH: Uncle Bill, do you mind just waiting in the kitchen, just—

BILL: I'd like to know who this is . . .

GLORIA: Oh Bill, I've heard a lot about you, /sorry to intrude—

BILL: This is—this is my boss, Gloria. Gloria, Bill Douaihy.

GLORIA: A pleasure, I'm sorry to intrude like this, I had a bit of a . . .
(*to* JOSEPH) . . . would he know what a panic attack /is?—

JOSEPH:	BILL:
I don't think so.	Did you offer her something to drink?

(*Under the dialogue below,* CHARLES *appears at the top of the stairs, unseen by* GLORIA *or* BILL. CHARLES *looks to* JOSEPH: "What is she doing here?" JOSEPH *indicates: "Get the hell back upstairs. Please. Please just go back upstairs."* CHARLES *rolls his eyes, upset, and exits up the stairs by the time* BILL *has said, "We're big fans of yours."*)

JOSEPH: No, she knows /this is a bad time.

GLORIA: Bill, don't worry about me, how are *you* doing, look at you.

BILL: I'm okay. You're the reason this one has health insurance, yes?
We're big fans of yours.

GLORIA: Oh, well . . . I'm a big fan of Joseph's . . . and of . . . all of this.

(JOSEPH's *cell phone rings.* GLORIA *picks up a snowman figurine.*)

. . . wow, what *is* this . . . ?

(JOSEPH's *cell rings again. He checks the caller ID.*)

JOSEPH: Ah, I need to take this, this is . . .

(JOSEPH *mouths "the doctor" to* BILL.)

JOSEPH (*to* GLORIA):   BILL:
I'm sorry, I've been waiting   Go ahead . . . we'll be fine.
for this call—You (*answering
the phone, walking to the
kitchen*) want something to
drink? Hello? . . .

GLORIA: Oh, I'd love a cup of coffee. Or wine.

JOSEPH (*on the phone*): . . . yes, yes . . . hold on, let me . . . (*getting settled at the kitchen table*) . . . I'm so glad you called back, I was told I'd have the results last week so I was—uh-huh . . . right . . . huh, okay . . . uh-huh . . . but that's . . . right, so then you think something's—oh, okay, okay . . . it just sounds like a big test to put someone through if . . . no, I get it, that's why I need to have it . . . yeah, okay, let me get a pen . . .

    (*Focus shifts to* GLORIA *and* BILL *on the couch.*)

GLORIA: I'll tell you, when you're depressed, the cold is actually a blessing, the bitter cold is. Because sometimes the feeling of . . . (*gestures to her stomach*) . . . that pit here . . . the only consolation I have is being outside and then coming into the warmth. Because suddenly . . . you go from being depressed and cold to something else . . . you're not better, but you are. Your body is pleased in spite of itself . . . you're aware of your vitality in a way you weren't before. It's so nice coming in out of the cold.

BILL: Would you like to go outside and come back in?

    (GLORIA *smiles.*)

GLORIA: I'm very sorry about your loss.

BILL: Thank you.

GLORIA: The holidays are hard, no?

BILL: The worst.

GLORIA: My husband . . . he passed away around this time, the anniversary's in a week, so the run-up to it's always . . . The day he died . . . I didn't think I'd live ten minutes.

(*Beat.*)

And when they told me he took his own . . . he let go of . . . from off of our balcony . . . I didn't think I'd live ten minutes past that whole [ordeal] . . . but time ticks . . . and there you are . . . you're someone new, I don't even know who . . .

(*Focus shifts to* CHARLES *and* VIN *staring at the picture of Saint Rafka.*)

VIN: She looks like an alien.

CHARLES: My dad insisted she was our guardian angel, always looking after our family. (*Sassy, to the picture*) And you're doing a fabulous job. Joseph used to have nightmares about her growing up, he'd dream she was standing over his bed with blood pouring out of her eyes.

VIN: Why was she a saint?

CHARLES: Oh . . . Rafka asked for suffering to get closer to God . . . and bam, she starts going blind, her joints got deformed—they couldn't figure out what was wrong with her . . . a doctor ended up ripping out her diseased eye *without anesthesia* . . .

VIN: Ah, gross . . .

CHARLES: And she was like, Bring. It. On.

(VIN *finds this funny in a you're such-a-massive-weirdo kind of way.* CHARLES *hands* VIN *a small framed photo.*)

This is her canonization. My dad wouldn't spend money to take us to Disney World, but in 2001 he boards a plane to Rome to watch John Paul II make her a saint. Big surprise the Lebanese get stuck with the patron saint of suffering, right?

VIN: Your dad looks like your brother.

(CHARLES *stares at the picture, a bit lost.*)

You okay?

CHARLES (*still staring at the photo*): Yeah, no . . . he does.

VIN: You need to get out of your head, gimme your hand.

CHARLES: Why?

(VIN *gestures for his hand . . .* CHARLES *isn't sure what he's doing.* VIN *takes his hand, starts an elaborate masculine handshake—*)

Oh—what, ah . . . ah . . . oh no . . .

(*The handshake continues . . .* CHARLES *is not adept at executing it.*

Back to JOSEPH *at the kitchen table on his cell. He has a pen and paper.*)

AUTOMATED VOICE (V.O.): . . . Welcome to the Department of Neurology at Lehigh Valley Hospital. This call may be monitored for security purposes. If this is a medical emergency, please press 1; for clinics, press 2; children's division, press 3; patient accounts, press 4; for directions and office hours, press 5; medical records, press 7; physician referrals, press 8 . . .

(*Focus shifts to* BILL *and* GLORIA *in midconversation.* GLORIA *has a glass of wine in her hand.*)

GLORIA: . . . and this was in the eighties, Bill, and my fibroid was so large, size of a melon, they just removed all the organs while they were in there, that's what they did back then, so . . . so kids were never a . . . and I coped with that, *I* did, therapy helped for a while, but now it's . . . I think it's . . . not having any . . .

(*Beat.*)

. . . my husband's family. I keep calling so they know . . . I don't want the fact that we're estranged to keep us from seeing each other. Did I tell you I'm estrang—

BILL: Yeah, no you did. Where the hell's Joseph?

GLORIA: . . . oh, do you need help with your—

BILL: No, no, /thank you, but—

GLORIA:—I forget what Joseph said—is it some sort of respiratory disease you have?—

BILL: No, and I'm—maybe I'm old-fashioned but . . . when did everyone become so comfortable talking about all their problems? In my family—and you say you admire Gibran, who—

GLORIA: Please, I'm honored to be in the presence of the bloodline—

BILL: That man didn't waste his life writing about his miseries, /and he had plenty—

GLORIA: Sure, but today, forget the silent suffering—his poverty, his ethnicity, that'd be his selling point.

BILL: No, the worst kind of pain—you can't share that, it's lonely, / it's—

GLORIA: Oh I [know]—yes, God . . . when I fell from grace—I'd published this love story, a memoir about a man who met his wife while he was imprisoned in a Nazi concentration camp . . .

BILL: Wow.

GLORIA: . . . precisely, and each day, his wife would disguise herself as a Christian farm girl and toss him a piece of fruit over the, you know, the big electrified fence at Auschwitz . . . well—turns out the author embellished the facts, the book was recalled, guess who took the fall, even though . . . would *you* know the height of a concentration camp wall?—or whether a young girl would lack the arm strength to hurl apples over it?—I'm not a detective, Bill. I wasn't at the Holocaust. There are only so many questions an editor can raise before she must trust and publish, or spike and fire.

BILL: I'm not sure I follow—

GLORIA: Anytime you try to put the truth on paper, you get a form of fiction. People don't want to accept that . . .

(*She pours herself another glass.*)

. . . but with your family, I know I can trust my sources.

BILL: What are we talking about?

GLORIA: Joseph's book. There was a sign in today's paper, look . . .

(GLORIA *shows* BILL *a section of the newspaper.*

Focus shifts to JOSEPH *in the kitchen, he's on his second call.*)

JOSEPH: . . . yeah, sure, but I don't want to schedule it unless . . . I *will* call the number on the back of my card, but even if my insurance covers seventy percent . . . but how much *is* a spinal tap so I can at least . . . yeah, wow, well I can't afford thirty percent of—

(*Beat.*)

—of course I have a credit card . . . no, yeah I know it's not your fault, I'll ask about a payment plan . . . uh-huh . . . fine, fine, let's book it . . . oh man, is there some way I can be discharged without—no no I just don't wanna pull my brother out of school if I don't have to . . .

BILL: Joseph!

JOSEPH: One minute!

VIN: Should you go check on your uncle?

CHARLES: No, he's fine.

BILL: Joseph!

VIN: Then why does he keep yelling?

CHARLES: I dunno but he can't make it up the stairs, let's stay here.

GLORIA:	BILL:
Joe!	Joseph!

CHARLES (*getting up*): Motherfucker . . .

JOSEPH: Give me one minute!

CHARLES (*calling downstairs*): Stop shouting, Uncle Bill!

BILL (*to* GLORIA): Excuse me . . .

JOSEPH (*entering the living room*): Hey . . . what's going on?

BILL: Come into the kitchen, please. You're writing a book about us?

GLORIA: Bill, don't forget to write down the date of that school board meeting for me.

BILL: I'll have Joseph give it to you.

JOSEPH: No, Gloria, that meeting's private /—we just want family there.

BILL: Joseph, give Gloria the address for the board meeting!

JOSEPH: Can you show yourself out? I'm sorry, I'll call you tonight—

GLORIA: Yes, just—(*showing him the paper*)—take a quick look at this photo: a man . . . his arm wrapped around his boys, comforting them in their moment of grief. And the caption:

JOSEPH: "Sons of the Prophet."

GLORIA: This is the cover and title of our book. Gibran is the Prophet. You're the focus but your father, brother, uncle, all the, all of the Mennonite /descendents—

JOSEPH: *Maronite—*

GLORIA:—right relatives from Lebanon, we could canvas the whole bloodline, hundreds of people offering new wisdom for a new day.

JOSEPH: These are polygamists.

GLORIA: We need to get a different print for your shirt . . . but the image is so moving.

BILL: Joseph!

GLORIA: I can pitch it to an editor at HarperCollins who owes me a favor.

(CHARLES *has made his way to the top of the stairs.*)

CHARLES: Hey, why does Uncle Bill keep shouting?

GLORIA: There's another Son of the Prophet.

CHARLES (*descending the stairs*): What's going on?	BILL: Joseph!
GLORIA: Hi, I'm Gloria.	JOSEPH: I'm coming . . .

CHARLES: Hey, I'm Charles.

GLORIA (*to* JOSEPH): Can he understand me?	BILL: Help me in the kitchen, Joseph . . .

JOSEPH: Where's Vin?—

CHARLES: He's fine.

JOSEPH: I asked you *where* he /is—

CHARLES: He can fucking take care of himself, /he's fine.

JOSEPH: *What's wrong with you,* we have company . . .

GLORIA: I'm a big girl . . .

BILL: Joseph!

GLORIA: Go, goodbye, Joe, I can show myself out . . .

JOSEPH: Thank you. (*To* CHARLES, *"Help me out."*) Please.

CHARLES (*understanding*): I got it.

> (JOSEPH *goes into the kitchen.* CHARLES *heads upstairs, then stops*—)

Hey, why did you call me a "Son of the Prophet"?

> (GLORIA *motions for* CHARLES *to join her on the couch; focus shifts to* BILL *and* JOSEPH.)

JOSEPH: Listen to me: no one will ever read this book, she's crazy, she has all this money from her dead husband, she gives me full health insurance just to keep her company—

BILL: You're not gonna exploit family tragedy—she wants to turn us into some circus show, full of untimely deaths—

JOSEPH: I wouldn't let her do that . . . the book will /never make it off the ground!

BILL: I don't want you working for her, I got lots of connections, we'll get /you another job—

JOSEPH: No, no, I'm keeping the job so I can see *real* doctors, not the brother of some state trooper you know in Archbald—

BILL: If this is how you talked to your father, it's no wonder his blood pressure was /through the roof—

JOSEPH: Or maybe it was 'cause you had him running around all day—you think he *liked* spending half his time at your place?

BILL: Oh that's good, now you can write about that in your book.

JOSEPH: Forget the book! There won't be a book!—

BILL: Then go out there and tell her /you won't—

JOSEPH: No, this is my house, don't tell me what to do. /Stop telling me what to do.

BILL: When I'm gone, you'll see who's been looking after you, I don't know who /you think—

JOSEPH: Who's looking after me now?! Who's taking care of me now?!—it's been a *nightmare* organizing you living here and you keep pretending like *you're* taking care of *us*!

(*Long beat.*)

BILL: I pray to St. Rafka every day for *you*. Not me.

(*Long beat.*)

I've been independent my whole life. It's a . . . [humbling thing]

(*Neither of them knows what to say, and neither wants to be the one to resolve the fight.*)

JOSEPH: I dunno if . . . we should discuss—maybe . . . another kind of home? . . . or . . . I dunno if, having the nurse come more often?—

BILL: Not that male nurse, Robert—

JOSEPH: Uncle Bill, /do you hear yourself? . . . okay, yeah, well . . . I'm out—

BILL: Don't stick me with him I still have scratches on my back and the guy won't shuttup, he just keeps talking to me—

(JOSEPH *heads for the back door in the kitchen.*)

Hey don't go out in this weather, sit down, please—

(JOSEPH *leaves. Focus shifts to* GLORIA *and* CHARLES *on the couch.* CHARLES *studies the newspaper photo.* GLORIA *thumbs through an atlas.*)

CHARLES: I would be the smaller kid?

(GLORIA *nods. Holds up the atlas to a page, her hand covers the name of the country.*)

GLORIA: Go.

CHARLES: French Guiana. Easy.

(*She searches for another page while* CHARLES *reads the newspaper article.*)

GLORIA: Go.

CHARLES: New York State upside down you're cheating /that's not even a country!

GLORIA: I am cheating you're too good! I grew up . . . here . . .

CHARLES: I can't wait to move to New York, I don't know why you'd ever leave, /no offense—

GLORIA: Oh, no, well I needed a . . . Manhattan is fabulous but . . . I'm not sure there's anything more . . . invisible in that city than a single, sixty-year-old woman.

(*Beat.*)

CHARLES: A single, seventy-year-old woman?

(CHARLES *smiles. So does* GLORIA.)

GLORIA: It was a wonderful place to grow up.

CHARLES: Yeah, where you're dropped off in the world, it's everything, /you know . . .

GLORIA: Location, location, location . . .

CHARLES: Yeah, Lebanon's suffered for *centuries* 'cause of its— (*pointing to the map of Lebanon*)—see how it's at the crossroads of three continents and religions and all these civilizations . . .

GLORIA: Hamas, Hizbollah . . . whole thing's a /mess . . .

CHARLES: . . . yeah, yeah no my grandparents . . . no one's life should have to be about finding . . . stability . . .

GLORIA: Yes, but whose life *isn't* . . . everyone starts life off with a certain number of handicaps, you hear what I'm saying—oh God, *can* you hear what I'm saying? /I didn't mean—

CHARLES: Oh, don't worry, /seriously, I can hear you . . .

GLORIA: I did not mean to offend you . . .

CHARLES: No, you didn't . . .

GLORIA: . . . I can't even tell which ear is more misshapen and . . .

CHARLES: What are you even . . .

GLORIA: . . . shrunken . . .

CHARLES: . . . saying?

GLORIA: . . . a little.

(GLORIA *convincingly answers a fake phone call.*)

Hello? . . . uh-huh . . .

(GLORIA *mouths "one second" to* CHARLES.)

BILL: Charles! Come in here, please . . .

GLORIA (*on the phone*): . . . okay great . . . uh-huh . . .

(CHARLES *walks to the kitchen where* BILL *is still seated.*)

CHARLES: Where's Joseph?

BILL: Tell Vin—the storm's terrible, get his parents' phone number, foster people, whoever, I'm gonna call them to check in. I should do that. He can sleep over in /the spare room.

CHARLES: My bedroom, wherever. Where'd Joseph go?

BILL: I don't know—

CHARLES: You don't know where /he is—

BILL: Can you just do what I asked!

>*(CHARLES is insulted BILL would yell at him. He walks back to the living room, heads for the stairs, wounded. GLORIA holds up another page in the atlas.)*

CHARLES: Eritrea.

GLORIA: Oh come on! I didn't even know Eritrea was a country.

CHARLES: The only one shaped like a martini glass . . . *(a depressed queen)* haaaay . . .

GLORIA: Look at that . . . come back here, where did you come up with that? . . .

CHARLES *(coming back down to sit with GLORIA)*: Oh my dad'd do these memory games all about how certain countries look like different animals or things . . . like how we all can draw Italy because it's a boot, right? . . . and . . . *(points to a page in the atlas)* . . . Lebanon looks like a man's face, in pain, screaming . . . see, if you just add an eye here . . . ?

GLORIA: Well, a man with . . . fetal alcohol syndrome, but yes . . .

CHARLES: The U.S. upside-down, it looks like an anteater. Alaska looks like Abraham Lincoln, the Aleutian Islands are his beard . . . Russia's a headless dog with its legs in the Caucasus Mountains, Japan looks like a snake . . .

GLORIA: Slow down, I like this—

>*(Focus slowly shifts to TIMOTHY's motel room. A knock at the door is heard.)*

CHARLES: . . . Romania's a fish . . . South Africa's a hippo . . .

>*(TIMOTHY opens the door. JOSEPH is outside.)*

JOSEPH: Hi . . .

CHARLES: Somalia's the number "seven" . . .

TIMOTHY (*shocked to see* JOSEPH): Hi . . .

GLORIA:—I'm writing all this down, I like this . . .

CHARLES: Slovenia's a chicken . . .

(*Lights go down on* CHARLES /GLORIA; *focus on* JOSEPH /
TIMOTHY.)

TIMOTHY: Whoa, /Hi—sorry what are you—

JOSEPH: Is this okay? The front desk gave me your room number.

TIMOTHY: What are you doing here?—

JOSEPH: I had to get out of my house, so . . . I . . . got in my car—

TIMOTHY: Are you still upset about . . . /'cause man, I'm so sorry—

JOSEPH: No, I'm . . .

(JOSEPH *shakes his head "no."*)

. . . I had to get out of my house and came here 'cause we never
got to discuss . . . when Mary Ingalls's blind husband regained
his sight? Remember how emotionally trying that was for her?
He could see her, but she couldn't see him?

TIMOTHY: That was very hard for Mary.

JOSEPH: I can go, if this is too [weird] . . .

TIMOTHY: No, sorry, I'm still just [shocked] . . . I mean, you're *here*—

JOSEPH: Am I crazy, or was there . . . I felt we had some kind of [con-
nection]— /that we had—

TIMOTHY: No, I felt that, I, definitely, but . . . no, yeah.

JOSEPH (*this has been bothering him*): Why don't you remember me from high school? Why don't you—

TIMOTHY: You set our course record twice, of course I remember you.

JOSEPH: Then why'd you /say—

TIMOTHY: I dunno . . .

JOSEPH: Tell me.

> (TIMOTHY *shakes his head "no."* JOSEPH *slowly moves in to embrace him.*)

TIMOTHY:—whoa, are . . . oh . . .

> (JOSEPH *holds him. He needed this. Long beat.*)

JOSEPH: If we do this, you can't cover my family's story.

TIMOTHY: If we—

> (JOSEPH *kisses his neck.*)

. . . oh . . . whoa . . . I should . . . (*losing himself*) . . . whoa . . . brush my teeth . . .

> (*The air is charged, their mouths meet. It's a tentative first kiss, two people following their attraction, drawing into each other. Beat.* JOSEPH *pulls* TIMOTHY's *shirt off.* TIMOTHY *follows suit, then goes for* JOSEPH's *belt buckle when* JOSEPH *pulls away.*)

TIMOTHY: What? We can slow down—

JOSEPH: No, just trying to think how I can get my pants off without you seeing my knee braces.

> (TIMOTHY *undoes* JOSEPH's *pants.* JOSEPH's *pants fall to the floor; he has on boxers and two knee braces.*)

TIMOTHY: You're a mess.

(*Beat.* JOSEPH *nods unsentimentally.* TIMOTHY *kisses him, they disrobe as the lights fade.* TIMOTHY *exits to the off-stage bedroom.* JOSEPH *kicks his shoes off, half-naked in the room as his nerves of sex transform into . . .*)

SCENE 5

ON FRIENDSHIP

(*. . . the nerves of a hospital visit. Another doctor's office. Another exam table.*

JOSEPH *receives a lumbar puncture (spinal tap). He lies on the table in the fetal position in a hospital gown while* DOCTOR MANOR *administers a needle into the base of his spine.* CHARLES *sits in the corner, observing.*)

DOCTOR MANOR: The worst part of the procedure is over, now we just wait until we collect 10 cc's of spinal fluid here. Any pain?

JOSEPH: No.

CHARLES: He's in a lot /of pain.

JOSEPH: She knows.

DOCTOR MANOR: If you think you might need someone to talk to about the stress—the hospital here has a support group for people with chronic pain, it's free. The delay in getting you a diagnosis is, it's Occam's Razor.

CHARLES: What's that?

DOCTOR MANOR: Just a theorem, reminds us the simplest answer is often the best. I mean the odds that someone like you, healthy, would suddenly get hit by three *unrelated* things—inflamed knees, neuropathy, muscle weakness—

JOSEPH: That's unlikely?

DOCTOR MANOR: Well, in medicine when you hear hoofbeats, you think horses not zebras. But the first round of tests is . . . (*examining her records*) . . . well if it's a horse, it's not a . . . Palomino . . . so now I'm thinking: okay, Lyme disease often causes the same kind of knee pain, whole host of neurological symptoms . . .

JOSEPH: Really?

DOCTOR MANOR: . . . yes, but you don't have Lyme disease according to your blood tests . . . (*studying the paperwork*) . . . it really would make sense for you to have Lyme disease. I'm hopeful the spinal fluid will give us some clues, see if there's some systemic inflammation—

JOSEPH: Could someone as healthy as me have something that serious?

DOCTOR MANOR: Well, you're *healthy* for someone who has a litany of medical problems. So that takes us to Hickam's Dictum.

CHARLES (*smiling*): Hickam's *Dick* /tum?—

JOSEPH: Don't.

DOCTOR MANOR: That's the theory that states "patients can have as many diseases as they damn well please." Let's see . . . (*Checks the container*) That took forever. Okay, needle's out.

> (DOCTOR MANOR *manages the containers of spinal fluid while* JOSEPH *sits up, grabs his head.*)

No lie down— /don't get up yet . . .

JOSEPH: Ow, /oh my God . . .

CHARLES: What happened, what's wrong?

DOCTOR MANOR: You're fine, about a third of patients experience migraines when they're upright after—I should have mentioned that at the start of the procedure. You need to stay on your back for at least thirty minutes here, okay? Just relax, I'll be back in a half hour.

(DOCTOR MANOR *exits.* JOSEPH *rolls onto his back.* JO-SEPH's *phone beeps.*)

JOSEPH: Just turn it off.

CHARLES (*reading the phone message*): "Libya looks like an ice cream cone with a bite taken out of it. xo Gloria."

JOSEPH: I've been getting texts like that all week.

CHARLES: She loves my idea.

JOSEPH: She's also fallen from grace, she's crazy.

CHARLES: Then quit.

JOSEPH: Who do you think's paying for this visit?

(*Beat.*)

I went out last night with Shane and Kim, just to keep ties, you know . . .

CHARLES: That's great—

JOSEPH: Yeah, no, I just should've—they chose Farley's which is all standing room at the bar, so my knees were flared and . . . they started up with—Grandpa needs to sit down . . . Grandpa whatever . . .

(*Beat.*)

CHARLES: Your friends aren't bad, they just don't know what to say, they don't know how to—like when Jesus was in the Garden.

JOSEPH: Oh my God . . .

CHARLES: . . . his Apostles didn't *want* to hurt /Him, but . . .

JOSEPH: Thank you, Father Charles—

CHARLES: . . . some things you can't understand until . . . you *understand* them. Until they're happening to you.

   (JOSEPH's *phone beeps.*)

JOSEPH: Give me the phone . . .

CHARLES (*reading the ID on the phone*): Timothy?

JOSEPH: Give me the phone!

CHARLES: Joseph, why would he be romantically interested in you? Your body is falling apart.

JOSEPH: He likes my personality—

CHARLES: You have a *terrible* personality, he's using you to get closer to the story—

JOSEPH: He's gonna stop covering it! And you're the one who told me to put myself out there, so don't—I can't be with you all the time. All is well, right? That's what that inspirational song you sent me /keeps saying—

CHARLES: Don't do that, you don't even know all the—the Rafka picture—it led me to that hymn, Joseph, to the words Dad said to us every day, so even if [it was random]—and that scripture passage matches Dad's birthday exactly: "My son . . . thine adversity and thine afflictions shall be but a small moment."—why do you need everything to be hopelessly random when—

JOSEPH: Because it is, because the chapter wasn't 12:17. It was 121:7. I looked it up—

CHARLES: If you move the colon—

JOSEPH: This isn't the *DaVinci Code*! Dad isn't sending you messages!

   (CHARLES *punches* JOSEPH *in the leg.*)

Ow!—what's your problem? . . .

(JOSEPH *sits up, blocks a second hit, pushes* CHARLES *away.*)

Motherfucker . . . What's your /problem?

(JOSEPH *grabs his head, lies back down.*)

Ahhhh . . .

CHARLES: What's *your* problem you're so /insensitive you are, and *cheap* just like Dad—

JOSEPH: Don't raise your voice—hey, relax, okay?

CHARLES:—you don't spend more than twenty bucks on anything, even *gifts* it's pathetic—

JOSEPH: Stop getting so upset—

CHARLES: I *am* upset you're having fluid drained from your spine!

JOSEPH: It's gonna be fine—

CHARLES: *No it's not we have no parents* . . . and Uncle Bill is *so old,* I keep hoping he dies so we can stop watching him get worse.

(CHARLES *cries, catches his breath.* CHARLES's *sensitivity always stirs anger in* JOSEPH; *but he knows he needs to say something. Long beat.* JOSEPH *looks toward* CHARLES, *whose head is buried in his hands.* JOSEPH *stares at the ceiling.*

Long beat.

Suddenly, DOCTOR MANOR *appears, her eyes glued to her charts.*)

DOCTOR MANOR: How's everyone doing?

JOSEPH:	CHARLES:
Good, yeah.	We're fine.

DOCTOR MANOR (*exiting, eyes on her chart*): Good, good, I'll be back in a bit.

(*She's gone. Long beat.* CHARLES *looks over at* JOSEPH, *whose eyes are now closed.*

Another very long beat.

Then another very long beat.)

CHARLES: Joseph.

(*Beat.*)

Joseph.

(*Beat.*)

Joe.

(*Beat.*)

Are you asleep?

(CHARLES *rolls his eyes.*)

Joseph.

CHARLES *approaches the table, concerned, nudges* JOSEPH's *arm.*

Jo—

(JOSEPH *jolts his whole body and opens his eyes, scaring the crap out of* CHARLES. *Successful ambush.* CHARLES *cannot believe* JOSEPH *would joke at a time like this.* JOSEPH *finds it very funny.* CHARLES *was so scared!* CHARLES *goes to smack* JOSEPH—*but* JOSEPH *grabs his arm, makes him laugh involuntarily through an arm restraint/tickling routine he's executed before. Finally,* JOSEPH *shows him some mercy.* CHARLES *moves away, still very upset.*

JOSEPH *loves how angry* CHARLES *is, finds it funny to watch him stew.* CHARLES *mulls about the room; eventually he sits back in the chair. He is still pissed.*

Beat.)

JOSEPH: When have *you* gotten anyone a gift over twenty bucks, your gifts are always *terrible.*

(*Beat.*)

You don't even *wrap* them.

(JOSEPH's *phone beeps.* CHARLES *goes to the phone.*)

CHARLES: "Western Sahara looks like a revolver. xo Gloria."

JOSEPH: Where is Western Sahara?

CHARLES: South of Morocco.

ON REASON & PASSION

(TIMOTHY *stands in a spotlight with a microphone, reporting.*)

TIMOTHY (*to the "camera"*): It all started out as a prank: steal a deer decoy, place it on a country road, and watch as motorists swerved to avoid it. It ended two weeks later when the victim—a custodian and father of two—suffered a fatal heart attack. When a judge ruled that the boy responsible for the mess could complete football season before serving his juvenile detention sentence, a seismic chasm cut through this typically tight-knit community. Tonight's debate centers around what one soccer mom calls "the merits and *demerits*" of instituting a rule that would allow school officials to sideline athletes convicted of criminal offenses. Our cameras aren't allowed inside but the meeting will be broadcast in its entirety on public access. We'll have our own assessment at eleven. Stay tuned . . .

> (*The audience is now the audience of a multipurpose room. Two female* SCHOOL BOARD MEMBERS *sit behind a simple long table with individual microphones. The Pennsylvania state flag stands off to the side.* JOSEPH, CHARLES, *and* BILL (*now in a wheelchair*) *sit in the front of the audience, off to the side.*)

BOARD MEMBER #1: . . . as you can see, board members Patrick Harding and Ed Larkin have removed themselves from tonight's vote, citing their association with the football team as booster club president and assistant coach, respectively, as uh, "an irreconcilable conflict of interest." We'll be proceeding nonetheless with the blessing of the . . .

BOARD MEMBER #1	BOARD MEMBER #2
(*doh-WAY-hees*):	(*duh-WHY-hees*):
Douaihys	Douaihys

BOARD MEMBER #1: and Superintendant Johnson, who's out there somewhere . . . And just because this is an open meeting—we're not tolerating any nonsense, no talking out of turn—youse'll all have a chance to voice your feelings during the open mic. We're grateful . . . the . . .

BOARD MEMBER #1	BOARD MEMBER #2
(*DUH-way-ees*):	(*duh-WHY-hees*):
Douaihys	Douaihys

BOARD MEMBER #1: wanted to be here today, I want to show them the respect they deserve. And uh, I believe Charles Douaihy wanted to read a statement. Charles?

(CHARLES *makes his way to the standing mic. The women's speeches cover the duration of time it takes* CHARLES *to reach the mic. The women sit back and speak softly, unaware their mics are still able to pick up their voices.*)

BOARD MEMBER #1:	BOARD MEMBER #2:
God love him he's got a hearing problem you know—he's deaf in one ear, Mrs. Laughney said . . .	What a trooper, God bless him . . .
	what kind of—? . . .
	God love him . . .
Is it Shirley who has Down's, God love her . . .	my cousin has Down's syndrome, that's no walk in the park . . . no, no Shirley just has a big forehead . . .

CHARLES (*reading his speech, into the mic*): We're all angry. There was no sense in what Vin did—he could have hurt any number of people. But it was my dad driving home that night. We'll never know why, or know if his heart attack was related to the accident—my family's gonna have to live with a lot of unanswered questions. I do know, I'm proud we don't want to channel our anger into stopping Vin from playing football. All my dad'd want us to ask is, can we learn from this? How can we hurt less? I hope Vin uses his talent to take him far, and I hope if he does play football, that this chance always reminds him of what he did, and informs his decision-making in the future. Thank you.

(As CHARLES *makes his way back to his seat, the* BOARD MEMBERS *"quietly" react. Their microphones are still on.*)

BOARD MEMBER #1:	BOARD MEMBER #2:
God bless him, to be so articulate . . . and gay . . . yeah, the both of them are, Mrs. Laughney said . . .	He's something, and no parents . . . . . . is he? . . . oh God love him . . . gay *and* hearing-impaired . . .

BOARD MEMBER #1: Thank you, Charles. Vin, if you'd like to read your essay?

(VIN *makes his way to the podium. His nervousness manifests in soft, fast, monotone speech free of correct emphasis.*)

VIN: In thinking about how much negative change my actions caused I also think about how going forward my actions can bring on just as much positive change going forward I pledge to do that with my actions the first action I took was last weekend with my teammates we did a coin drop and raised money for something Mr. Douaihy would have appreciated according to his son money for the Maronite families who have been coming over from Lebanon because of the war the cash was given to the

Douaihys' church the head priest agreed to handle getting it out to the families one thing I want to be clear about is that if football gets taken from me I respect whatever gets decided here today and I mean that in closing I want to

(VIN *loses his place for a few seconds—*)

BOARD MEMBER #1: Do /you—oh, okay . . .

VIN: end not with my own words which will always fall short but to show respect for Mr. Douaihy I'm going to read a prayer to his favorite saint which I found on the Internet.

(*Takes out the prayer from his pocket. The simple action of having to dig something out of his pocket allows him to catch his breath a bit.*)

"Prayer to Saint Rafka. We ask you to spread joy in our world which is suffering; teach us to live peacefully. Your own pain couldn't be cured in your lifetime, so you embraced it and allowed others to wipe away your tears. Now we ask you to wipe away our tears; cure sick people; comfort sad people; fill people's hearts with joy and love.

(*Beat.* VIN*'s lost his place.*)

/Amen."

BOARD MEMBER #1: Thank—oh, Amen, thank you Vin, why don't you take a seat.

BOARD MEMBER #2: Did you /understand that first part?

BOARD MEMBER #1:	BILL:
It's fine, let him sit down.	I should have a chance to say something.
CHARLES:	JOSEPH:
/Uncle Bill, be quiet . . .	Don't say a word, I'm serious.

VIN (*to the family*): I'm really sorry.

BOARD MEMBER #1:	BOARD MEMBER #2:
What's he saying?	Charles—what's the problem?

JOSEPH:
There's no problem . . . please,
Uncle Bill . . .

BILL:
I'm saying /I'd like to say
something, that's all. Can I
have the microphone? Let me
say this . . .

BOARD MEMBER #1:
Vin, you can /step away from
the mic . . . yeah, no it's okay,
you can go back to your
seat please . . .

JOSEPH (*to* BOARD MEMBER #2):
No, just ignore him, I'm
sorry—he's fine, don't—

VIN:
Should I stand or just—
I think he's still
talking to me . . . ?

BOARD MEMBER #2 (*to* CHARLES):
Here, give this to him . . .
here . . . (*to* JOSEPH)
. . . it's okay . . .

(*She passes the mic to* BILL. BILL *doesn't have the oxygen to shout.*)

BILL: Vin.

(VIN *stands up from his seat.*)

I know you meant well with that speech, okay? But I *don't* know that my brother'd want you to have another chance. Look at me.

(*Beat.*)

So if you play in that championship game—look at me, please. If you get a second chance and I see you on that field playin' like some faggy-ass halfback, not doing your best—

(*At the word "faggy,"* JOSEPH /CHARLES *bury their heads in embarrassment.*)

Don't ever forget my brother . . . because the Douaihys, we're part of history, we're gonna fade if you don't remember . . . /*Marune* [I am Maronite] . . .

JOSEPH (*taking the mic from* BILL): It's okay . . .

(*Under* BILL's *line below,* JOSEPH *hands the mic back to* BOARD MEMBER #2 *and silently apologizes to* VIN *on his way back.*)

BILL: . . . we came from France, we were knights, this is before the Crusades . . . dammit . . .

CHARLES: Restroom? /I got it . . .

JOSEPH: I'll take you, /hold on . . .

BOARD MEMBER #1: I think we could all do with a brief recess, yes? /Motion to regroup?

BOARD MEMBER #2: Yes, we could. Second . . .

BOARD MEMBER #1: We'll take a five-minute recess.

(JOSEPH *starts to wheel* BILL *out—they both see* TIMOTHY *approaching.*)

CHARLES: No, I got it. Joseph.

JOSEPH: No I got—

CHARLES: Joseph. I can do it. Okay?

JOSEPH (*nodding, appreciative*): Let's meet in the car, we don't need to stick around— /I'll tell them we're going.

BILL: Are you gonna take me to the bathroom or what?

CHARLES:—yes, Impatient, I'm taking you.

TIMOTHY: Hey guys . . . (*to* BILL) . . . *Marhaba, kifak* [Hi, how are you?], Mr. Douaihy?

CHARLES (*over his shoulder, to* TIMOTHY): It's completely obvious you're a homosexual—

JOSEPH: *Goodbye,* Charles.

(CHARLES *wheels* BILL *out.*)

TIMOTHY: Hey—my editor wants me to get a few pictures with my camera phone, but—

JOSEPH: Are you kidding me?—

TIMOTHY: What?—no I'm asking because I won't take them unless you approve—

JOSEPH: We're not having this conversation.

(JOSEPH *moves away,* TIMOTHY *follows him.*)

TIMOTHY: You won't return my calls. Hey—I care about you—I got an offer from ABC based on this coverage, if I walk away it'd look terrible.

JOSEPH: You couldn't find a family more tragic than mine to exploit?—

TIMOTHY: *You came to my hotel room,* so don't—I can't hole myself up like you—

JOSEPH: You don't see the responsibilities I'm saddled with?— between my brother and my uncle—you think /I *want* [to be saddled with them?]—

TIMOTHY: I think you're scared to leave your own backyard, it's why—it's not an attractive quality—it's like you're *looking* to suffer—

JOSEPH: This coming from the entitled purveyor of more grief porn /than—

TIMOTHY: So you aren't privileged, boo-hoo, pull yourself up by your own fucking bootstraps and do something with your life.

You can't afford to travel the world, fine—but *you haven't even been to Connecticut.* Rent a car and drive to the Delaware Water Gap, do *something*—

JOSEPH: You are so delusional—

TIMOTHY: How am I—

JOSEPH: Do you really think you understand people's pain /in some special way?—

TIMOTHY: You don't know what I've been through—

JOSEPH: No, I just know you like to spend holidays in some kinda ghetto even though your dad owns /Mount Airy Lodge—

TIMOTHY: Because my mom, my mom *was* born into poverty, that's not a /lie—

JOSEPH: You said she grew up down the block from us in Marvin Apartments.

TIMOTHY: That is a poor development.

JOSEPH: It's *middle-income housing!*

(*The* BOARD MEMBERS *walk back in, talking to each other indiscernibly.* VIN *wanders back in.* JOSEPH *and* TIMOTHY *are more cautious with their conversation.*)

TIMOTHY: You want to talk about delusional, who's the one suffering from all these mysterious aches and pains? . . .

(*This almost knocks the wind out of* JOSEPH.)

JOSEPH: You think I'm making it up?—

TIMOTHY: Do you have a diagnosis? Do you?

BOARD MEMBER #1: We're gonna start up again—

TIMOTHY (*seeing how hurt* JOSEPH *is*): Sorry, just—you don't look sick.

JOSEPH: You don't look like an asshole.

BOARD MEMBER #2:	BOARD MEMBER #1
Is he okay?	(*concerned*):
	Joseph?

TIMOTHY (*to* BOARD MEMBER #2): He's fine . . .

JOSEPH: And I'm moving my uncle into a *home,* thanks for asking, /it's been rough.

BOARD MEMBER #2:	TIMOTHY:
Are you okay, Joseph? You	. . . yeah he's, no no, he's fine,
don't have to stay.	he just needs some air . . .
JOSEPH (*to* TIMOTHY):	BOARD MEMBER #1
I'm not fine. I'm *not* fine.	(*to* BOARD MEMBER #2):
	Let's just move on, he'll
	[figure out we've started] . . .

TIMOTHY (*uncomfortable, to* JOSEPH): Yeah, well, you're making a scene.

JOSEPH: Yeah, well, your dick's unusually small.

(JOSEPH *walks away from* TIMOTHY, *starts to exit.*)

VIN (*raising his hand*): Should I be sticking around, or—

BOARD MEMBER #1:	BOARD MEMBER #2:
Yes, sit down.	Don't go anywhere.

BOARD MEMBER #1 (*into the mic*): Okay everyone, we're gonna move on to the open mic /portion of the . . . ma'am, we're about to . . . I guess we've . . . started, I guess . . .

(GLORIA *approaches the standing mic at the foot of the stage from the audience. Her voice stops* JOSEPH, *who was about to leave.*)

GLORIA: Gloria Gurney, originally from Manhattan, currently re-
siding in Nazareth . . . oh, should I wait? /I'm sorry . . .

BOARD MEMBER #1: . . . no, it's fine just, everyone needs to limit
their comments to three minutes, okay?

GLORIA: . . . all right . . . I'm here today in support of this incredible
family here.

(GLORIA *wobbles a bit, feels faint.*)

BOARD MEMBER #1:	BOARD MEMBER #2:
Is she all right?	Oh my God . . .

GLORIA (*into the mic*): . . . I'm fine, I'm saying . . . what the Douaihys
have lost is . . . none of us can know . . . I'm here because this
morning I was struck with . . . a sense of . . . not *understanding* but . . . being a *part* of your family, Joseph . . . not by blood,
but . . .

(BOARD MEMBERS *attempt to approach* GLORIA, *who
wards them off. The following, despite* GLORIA's *state, is
not full of histrionics. In her own way, she's more lucid
than we've ever seen her. It's real sentiment.*)

. . . no, I'm fine, I'm saying . . . I've lost family . . . I know how . . .
people leave you . . . they love you, they leave you and then . . .
in a flash . . . happiness . . . becomes this . . . thing . . . in *other*
people's eyes . . . it's . . .

JOSEPH:	BOARD MEMBER #1:
Gloria . . .	Can you join me outside in the hall, ma'am?

GLORIA: . . . I don't know why some people's lives are full of . . . getting scraped down . . . it's unknowable, but this morning I felt . . .
not just my sadness . . . (*looks to* JOSEPH) . . . it was yours . . . (*to
the audience*) . . . all of ours. We're not strangers. We know each
other well. We know each other well.

(GLORIA *wipes away tears. Everyone's thinking: That was kind of a deranged and beautiful thing to say. Long beat.*)

BOARD MEMBER #2: Is she *high?*

BOARD MEMBER #1:	BOARD MEMBER #2:
Ma'am, please step away from the mic.	I'll call 9-1-1 . . .

(BOARD MEMBER #1 *attempts to gently escort* GLORIA *away.* GLORIA *sees* JOSEPH *approaching the stage.*)

GLORIA:	BOARD MEMBER #1:
No, no, Joseph will take care of me . . .	. . . okay . . . you're okay . . .

JOSEPH: What are you doing here?

(JOSEPH *starts to guide* GLORIA *off the stage. He motions to the* BOARD MEMBERS, *"It's okay, I'll help her."*)

GLORIA: I got scared, /I was alone after—HarperCollins said "no" to me, they said maybe the geography idea if I wasn't involved . . .

JOSEPH: Yeah, okay . . . but I asked you not to come . . . okay . . . okay, c'mon . . . okay . . .

GLORIA: . . . as if there'd be a book proposal without me . . .

JOSEPH: It was my *father's* idea—

GLORIA: . . . I know, no I'm saying we know /each other well, Joe—

JOSEPH: No you don't know my father well, okay?

GLORIA: . . . we're like family, we're together /in this—

JOSEPH: No we're not what's wrong with you *take care of yourself.* We're alone.

(*Beat. Everyone is riveted. The flash of* TIMOTHY's *Black-berry camera goes off. He's hideously embarrassed, wasn't planning on anyone knowing he was taking a picture.*)

TIMOTHY:
Oh shit . . . /sorry, sorry . . .

GLORIA:
Joe, where are you—Joe . . .

BOARD MEMBER #1:
Please no flash photography.

BOARD MEMBER #2:
Who's taking pictures?

(*Something's cracked open for* JOSEPH *. . . he's not sure what, but he wants to get out of the auditorium. He leaves* GLORIA, *walks toward* TIMOTHY.)

GLORIA: . . . wait, let's go back to the office so /we can—

JOSEPH: No, I quit.

(JOSEPH *takes* TIMOTHY's *phone and throws it against the wall, smashing it to pieces. Without stopping,* JOSEPH *continues toward the back of the auditorium.*)

GLORIA: No, /no, Joe I need you to help me get home . . . Joe, please . . .

BOARD MEMBER #2:
I think we're going to take another recess—everyone just take ten . . .

BOARD MEMBER #1:
Ma'am, I'm going to help you offstage, call the police— come on . . . you're okay, you're okay . . .

(JOSEPH *continues toward the exit.* BOARD MEMBER #1 *approaches to help* GLORIA, *takes her arm—*TIMOTHY *recovers the pieces of his phone, shocked.*)

GLORIA: Joe, please—I need you to help me get home!

(JOSEPH—*at the back of the auditorium—is flat-out exasperated* GLORIA *can't figure this out for herself.*)

JOSEPH: *Take a fucking taxi!*

(JOSEPH *exits. The* BOARD MEMBERS *help* GLORIA *offstage.*)

ON YESTERDAY & TODAY

(*Physical therapy. The boardroom table has been trans-*
formed: it now has a few wads of brightly colored putty
and weights on it.

JOSEPH *is in the middle of a basic arm stretch (an ulnar*
nerve glide), just as we met him in the opening scene.
He's clearly in a better place, calm.

MRS. MCANDREW, *sixties, approaches his table, sits. She*
starts squeezing and manipulating a wad of putty. She
notices him.)

MRS. MCANDREW: Joseph?

JOSEPH: Oh, hey, Mrs. McAndrew—

MRS. MCANDREW: Thought it was you, I saw your picture in the
paper a few years ago when you won the Steamtown Marathon,
congrat /ulations—

JOSEPH: Thanks, thank you.

(*Beat.*)

We got your card and the flowers, that was real nice—

MRS. MCANDREW: You get to be my age it becomes a ritual, reading
the obituaries, so . . . my heart broke for you boys.

(*Beat.*)

You still running?

JOSEPH: No. Actually, you knew me in my prime. Kindergarten was a good year for me. Chocolate milk every day, He-Man lunch box . . . it's kinda all been downhill after that.

MRS. MCANDREW: Physical therapy makes you *feel* like you're back in kindergarten, doesn't it?

JOSEPH: Oh, yeah.

(*Beat.*)

MRS. MCANDREW: Is it terrible if I tell you . . . I saw that clip of you at the board meeting—

JOSEPH: Ah, /you saw that?

MRS. MCANDREW: My granddaughter showed it to me online and . . .

JOSEPH: Yup, /yes . . .

MRS. MCANDREW: . . . she said it had over ten thousand hits.

JOSEPH: And growing, I'm told . . .

MRS. MCANDREW: "Take a fucking taxi." Said that to my husband this morning. Oh and Kay Hoban told me about that geography book you're doing /. . . sounds great . . .

JOSEPH: Oh yeah, HarperCollins is giving us forty-five thousand bucks to develop it, which isn't a whole lot, but . . .

MRS. MCANDREW: It's not nothing.

JOSEPH: No. Gloria got, 'cause of that video footage, she got a six-figure book deal to disclose the details of her husband's suicide, so . . .

MRS. MCANDREW (*shakes her head, disapproving, then*—): I'm gonna read that, I should admit that now.

JOSEPH: To make it in this country, you either need to be an extraordinary human being . . . or make a series of extraordinarily bad life-decisions. All of us in the middle, we're not worth so much.

MRS. MCANDREW: Forty-five thousand.

JOSEPH: True, forty-five thousand.

(MRS. MCANDREW *begins to twist a yellow-netted rubber thing.* JOSEPH *rolls out some putty.*)

MRS. MCANDREW (*holds up her wrist*): My son convinced me to go skiing.

JOSEPH: Oh, sprained something.

(*Beat.*)

MRS. MCANDREW: You know, I can still picture your mom, God love her, because she always walked you right to your desk in the morning—

JOSEPH: Yeah, 'cause I wouldn't stop crying, I was such a baby. I have these clear memories of being so scared, and then . . . end of the day, I'm just . . . walking home, telling her about an art project or—do you still do that worksheet with all the numbers inside the bear's belly?

MRS. MCANDREW: Kids love that worksheet, and it's just—would adding numbers inside a bear's belly give you any joy today?

JOSEPH: None.

MRS. MCANDREW: It's amazing, those handful of things that lodge in your brain when you're young. My granddaughter asked me what toys I had when I was her age, she's five—and the first thing that comes into my mind is this memory of when my teacher asked us to name healthy breakfast foods and I raised my hand and said: plain doughnuts. Plain doughnuts.

JOSEPH: There's lots of unhealthy things you can *add* to a doughnut, I respect your answer.

MRS. MCANDREW: I lost sleep over that . . . if only I knew what real problems were headed my way. I lost my mom and dad last year, couple months apart.

JOSEPH: I'm sorry.

MRS. MCANDREW: They lived long lives, I have nothing to complain about, especially compared to what you boys have been through.

JOSEPH: No, you don't have to—I'm in this, like a group for—nevermind, it's just . . . it's funny how you can get in the habit of belittling your own [experiences]—I mean, 'cause things can *always* be worse . . .

MRS. MCANDREW: Well you also can't stand in your pain too long, it's like quicksand, you'll sink, never get past it.

JOSEPH: Can you get past something that doesn't go away?

MRS. MCANDREW: I don't know [that] it *does* go away, but . . . I've been around a while, so I've seen it shift into . . . maybe . . . more compassion? or just a . . . an awareness that . . .

JOSEPH: What?

MRS. MCANDREW: . . . that we wouldn't have otherwise? Our bodies break so easily, but they're so *resilient,* you know? We can use reminders—

JOSEPH: Not sure that /I—

MRS. MCANDREW: Well I also believe in Jesus Christ but I'm trying not to sound like a religious nut.

JOSEPH: You're all right. I miss having my dad's faith around even though I don't subscribe to it. I miss *him.*

(JOSEPH's emotions catch him off guard, he starts crying. She notices.)

MRS. McANDREW: Oh, Joe . . .

JOSEPH: Sorry, I'm just . . . (difficult admission) . . . not doing good. It's been a bad year.

MRS. McANDREW: I'm so sorry.

(JOSEPH takes a deep breath, recovers.)

JOSEPH: I didn't sprain something. I have to go see this, some other specialist at UPenn, whole thing's a mess.

MRS. McANDREW: I hope you find some relief soon.

JOSEPH: Thanks. Glad you know, 'cause I have to do some nerve glides now and . . . doing them in front of people is . . . [completely humiliating] . . .

MRS. McANDREW: Do you see what I'm working with here?

(She holds up the yellow-netted rubber thing she's been twisting. JOSEPH begins his nerve glides.)

(Recognizing the exercise) I had to do that one. If you do it in time with the music, it goes by faster.

(MRS. McANDREW demonstrates as the background music becomes prominent.

JOSEPH watches her. He never thought of that. He joins her.

The music grows. The rhythm is simple, slow, mellow, steady, like a heartbeat. The space feels a bit bigger, more open. They look out—not smiling—but in sync, their arms moving in time with the music as the curtain falls.)